RECENT REVOLUTIONS IN BIOLOGY

RECENT REVOLUTIONS IN BIOLOGY

James A. Corrick

FRANKLIN WATTS 1987
NEW YORK   LONDON
TORONTO   SYDNEY
A SCIENCE IMPACT BOOK

Diagrams by Vantage Art, Inc.

Photographs courtesy of: © Lynn McLaren/Photo Researchers: p. 12; Brookhaven National Laboratory, Photography Division, Upton, New York: pp. 15, 46; Carolina Biological Supply Company: p. 19; Nelson L. Max, © 1983 by the Regents of the University of California: p. 22. Louise T. Chow and Thomas R. Broker, University of Rochester: p. 25; © Don W. Fawcett/Photo Researchers: p. 27; © Keith R. Porter/ Photo Researchers: p. 29; © Lee D. Simon/Photo Researchers: p. 34; Genex Corporation: p. 38; Keiichi Namba and Donald L.D. Casper, Brandeis University and Gerald Stubbs, Vanderbilt University: p. 52; Burndy Library: p. 55 (top); © George Holton/Photo Researchers: pp. 55 (bottom), 57; Harvard University News Office, Cambridge, MA: p. 61; Field Museum of Natural History, Chicago: p. 71; Natural History Museum of Los Angeles County, News Media Relations Office: p. 76; National Oceanographic and Atmospheric Administration: p. 77; Jessie Cohen, Office of Graphics and Exhibits, National Zoological Park, Smithsonian Institution: p. 84 (top); Francie Schroeder, National Zoological Park, Smithsonian Institution (1976): p. 84 (bottom); National Zoological Park, Smithsonian Institution: p. 85; Dr. Robert Ballard, Woods Hole Oceanographic Institute: p. 91; John Baross: pp. 92, 93; S. C. Delaney/EPA: p. 100; © Carl Frank/Photo Researchers: p. 105; © Colin G. Butler, F.R.P.S./Photo Researchers: p. 109; North Carolina Zoological Park, Asheboro, NC: p. 113.

Library of Congress Cataloging-in-Publication Data

Corrick, James A.
Recent revolution in biology.

(A Science impact book)
Bibliography: p.
Includes index.
Summary: Surveys new theories, discoveries, and realms of inquiry in biology, discussing evolution, gene therapy, genetic engineering, life on other planets, and other topics.
1. Biology—Juvenile literature. [1. Biology]
I. Title. II. Series.
QH308.7.C67 1987   574   86-22464
ISBN 0-531-10341-2

Copyright © 1987 by James A. Corrick
All rights reserved
Printed in the United States of America
6 5 4 3

*TO PERRI, IN FULFILLMENT
OF A PROMISE MADE LONG AGO,
AND TO RICHARD—A BOOK
FOR THE COLLECTION*

OTHER BOOKS BY JAMES A. CORRICK

THE HUMAN BRAIN: MIND AND MATTER
RECENT REVOLUTIONS IN CHEMISTRY

CONTENTS

CHAPTER 1
11 LOOKING INTO LIFE

CHAPTER 2
17 OPENING UP THE CELL

CHAPTER 3
32 UNCOILING THE DOUBLE HELIX

CHAPTER 4
45 TAKING THE MEASURE OF LIFE

CHAPTER 5
54 DISCOVERING THE WAYS OF CHANGE

CHAPTER 6
67 SCRUTINIZING THE FOSSIL RECORD

CHAPTER 7
80 ESTABLISHING THE NEW ORDER

CHAPTER 8
89 FINDING NEW LIFE

CHAPTER 9
99 TRACING THE WEB OF LIFE

CHAPTER 10
108 LOOKING FROM THE INSIDE OUT

116 GLOSSARY

121 SELECTED READING

124 INDEX

RECENT REVOLUTIONS IN BIOLOGY

CHAPTER 1
LOOKING INTO LIFE

*I*n one sense, we are all biologists. We are fascinated by living things, and we are surrounded by them daily. The birds that sit in rows on power lines or on ledges of buildings. The butterflies that flit from bush to bush. The lightning bugs that blink mysteriously in spring lawns. Our cats and our dogs that provide both company and entertainment. Our houseplants that provide a feeling of life to our homes. Even ourselves.

There are few of us who do not relish a trip to the zoo and who have not watched spiders in their webs or fish swimming in pet store aquariums. Most of us are interested in other living things.

How do they live? Why do they act the way they do? How did they get the way they are? These are questions that we naturally ask ourselves about animals and plants, and we should not be surprised that these are a few of the questions professional biological scientists have been asking—as well as attempting to answer—for centuries.

THE SCIENCE OF LIFE

Biology is the science of life, and its goal is the complete understanding of living creatures. It studies their behavior, their structure, their chemical nature, their relationships to one another and to their surroundings. It looks at the way living things have evolved from their remote ancestors, and it looks at the way they pass present characteristics on to their offspring.

Diversity in nature. Compare this photograph with the one of a rain forest in Chapter 9.

You do not have to be a biologist to recognize that one of the fundamentals of life is its diversity. There are hundreds of thousands of different types of insects, thousands of different sorts of fish, and thousands of different kinds of birds. There are organisms—**microorganisms**—so small you require a microscope to see them, while other creatures, such as the blue whale, are so large they are bigger than many houses.

This very diversity has given rise to many of the fields of biology. You will find biological scientists, botanists, who study only plants, and others, zoologists, who are interested solely in animals. Biochemists are concerned only with the chemical processes of living things, and ecologists are interested in the complex interrelationships that exist among all living organisms. Some of these divisions of biology, such as sociobiology, might seem better to belong to some other field, such as psychology. But the study of animal behavior has become increasingly important in the last few years—some of the findings may allow us to understand human behavior more fully.

Despite the great diversity of biology, certain properties are common to all living things. First, all organisms need energy to live. Plants obtain this energy directly from the sun, while animals obtain it from eating plants and other animals—their energy is secondhand.

Second, both plants and animals use this energy to replace and repair their structures. They also use this energy to keep their internal chemical systems functioning at a constant and consistent level, for if such systems produce too little or too much, the organism dies.

Third, all living things are the products of **evolution.** This is the process by which earlier, often simpler life-forms gave rise through physical and chemical changes to the newer, generally more complex organisms of today.

Fourth, all organisms are composed of one or more basic units called **cells.** Each cell is a little chemical factory in which all the chemical processes that keep living things alive are carried out.

It is the existence of these common features of life that underlies all biological studies. Such similarities allow researchers to study one life-form and then to apply their findings to many other living things.

OUR BIOLOGICAL HERITAGE

Biology has always been important to the human race. Our remote ancestors—long before they learned to write and keep records—required a basic biological knowledge to avoid poisonous plants and to know the behavior patterns of predators. Later, but still before the invention of writing, humans used their biological knowledge to domesticate animals and to develop food crops. The birth of agriculture was one of the greatest of all human revolutions.

Until comparatively recently, the major focus of biologists was the whole organism—the individual animal or plant. The reason for this was simple: they were easily visible for study. In some cases, although rarely, entire animal and plant populations were objects of interest. The result of all this research produced many valuable observations as well as an initial classification system that placed living organisms into related groups and subgroups. It also produced Darwin's Theory of Evolution.

It was not until the invention of reliable, sophisticated microscopes in the nineteenth century, however, that biologists turned their attention to another level of biology—the study of the cell. Thus began the first true understanding of how living things functioned.

MOLECULAR BIOLOGY

But the cell was not far enough. To be able to understand how the cell did its chemical duty, to understand how parents could pass on characteristics to offspring, and to find the true basis of life required a further breakthrough—a breakthrough on the molecular level.

All matter is composed of atoms, and most atoms are found in atomic combinations called molecules. A molecule of water is made up of two atoms of hydrogen and one atom of oxygen.

Living things are no different from nonliving matter: they

The controlled-environment growth chamber at Brookhaven National Laboratory, where a biologist is studying the effects of acid rain on plants

are made up of atoms, and these atoms are found in molecules. In the first quarter of the twentieth century, biologists were able to begin studying life at the molecular level. Such research is the basis for one of the most recent biological revolutions, **genetic engineering,** the actual manipulation of the genetic material DNA.

The greatest effect of the molecular revolution was a new way of looking at living organisms. Prior to our century, biologists looked at the entire organism and tried to work backward in order to understand life. Such an approach, although it accumulated a great deal of useful data, provided only a tantalizingly incomplete understanding of biological mechanisms. For this reason, biologists were unable to explain the actual effect of evolutionary pressure on living things—what was it in plants and animals that actually changed and why? Nor were they able to explain biological inheritance, heredity.

—15

Now, with the molecular revolution, biologists no longer looked from the large to the small, but from the small to the large. Biology's hierarchy was now the molecule, the cell, the organism, and the population. In recent years, this molecular revolution has become all pervasive. We shall see its effect on the recent revolutions in contemporary DNA research, evolutionary theory, cellular studies, even the reclassification of the whole spectrum of living things.

THE POPULATION QUESTION

Although pre-twentieth-century biologists occasionally studied entire populations of plants and animals, such research was rare. In our century, the same century that saw the molecular revolution, we also see a growing interest in population biology, the study of animal and plant populations.

Faster and more reliable transportation has made such studies—which often must be carried out over large areas of land and sea—more practical than in past centuries. Further, in the last half century, there has been a growing awareness of the importance of population studies not only in understanding evolution but also in learning about the complex web of life that spans the entire earth. Additionally, the recognition of humanity's place in this web continues to this day to be part of the fuel that drives the environmental revolution.

It is obvious looking at these fields of late twentieth century biology that the modern biologist must be more than just knowledgeable about plants, animals, and microorganisms. He or she must often be a good chemist, a good physicist, a good geologist, even a good sociologist. Although fieldwork—actually going out and studying organisms in their natural habitats—still plays a major role in biological research, a great deal of a biologist's time is spent in the laboratory surrounded by computer-assisted analytical instruments. Indeed, a significant number of modern biologists never set aside the lab coat for the boots and work pants of the field.

So let us now look at the new biology and the new biologists. Let us see what biology is doing today, what it is discovering, and what its future may be.

CHAPTER 2
OPENING UP
THE CELL

THE LIFE FACTORY

The factory never closes; for it, there are no holidays. Each day, it manufactures thousands, sometimes millions, of complex, precise products. Unlike most factories, it uses many of these products for its own maintenance and operation. It is the living cell.

To understand the molecular revolution that has led to genetic engineering, we must first understand about the cell, that basic unit of all living matter. Indeed, the understanding of all organisms begins with the cell. In the cell, all the molecular activities needed to support life, to grow, to reproduce occur. Cells are the factories of life, and as we shall see in the next chapter, genetic engineering is starting to allow biologists to manage and direct those factories. Cells range in size from 0.00000004 inch (0.0000001 centimeter) across—those of the smallest microorganisms—to 3 inches (8 centimeters)—the yolk of an ostrich egg. Despite this latter example, it requires a microscope to see most cells.

The number of cells in an organism can range from one to several million. The cell of one-celled organisms, such as amoebae and bacteria, is unspecialized. It can take up and use food from its surroundings. It can process waste and excrete it. It can reproduce. And, usually, it can move.

On the other hand, multicelled organisms—plants and animals—have cells that are almost always specialized. In our bodies, we have cells that contract so that we can move. We have other cells that can absorb the food we eat. None of these cells can exchange functions. A muscle cell cannot transmit nerve impulses. A nerve cell cannot contract and move.

INSIDE THE CELL

All cells are surrounded by a membrane (see Figure 1) that allows some chemicals to enter. Unlike animal cells, plant cells also have a cell wall that makes them rigid.

Except for certain microorganisms, such as bacteria, the cells of all living things have a central structure called the nucleus. The nucleus contains the cell's **chromosomes,** which come in pairs and hold the cell's **genes,** the elements in a cell controlling heredity. When a cell reproduces itself, it creates a duplicate of each of its chromosomes so that the daughter cells are exactly like the parent cell.

The remainder of the cell is filled with a substance called cytoplasm. This jelly-like material is a complex mixture of various chemicals, both liquids and solids, all suspended in water. The exact composition of cytoplasm varies from ani-

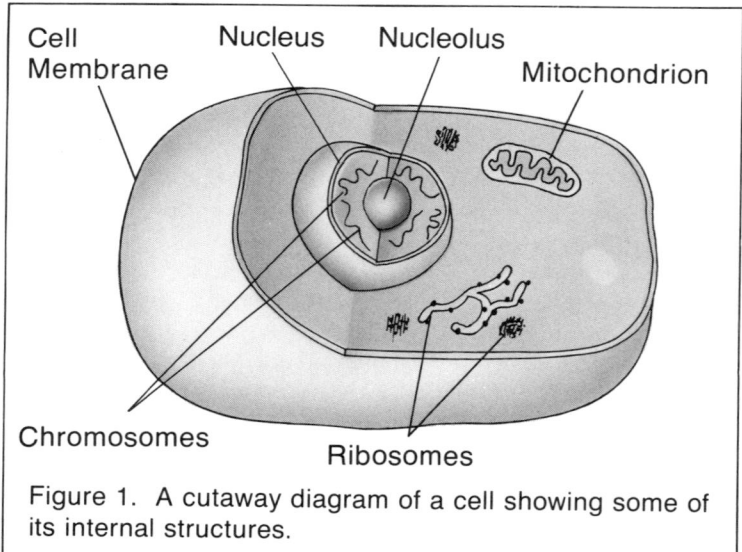

Figure 1. A cutaway diagram of a cell showing some of its internal structures.

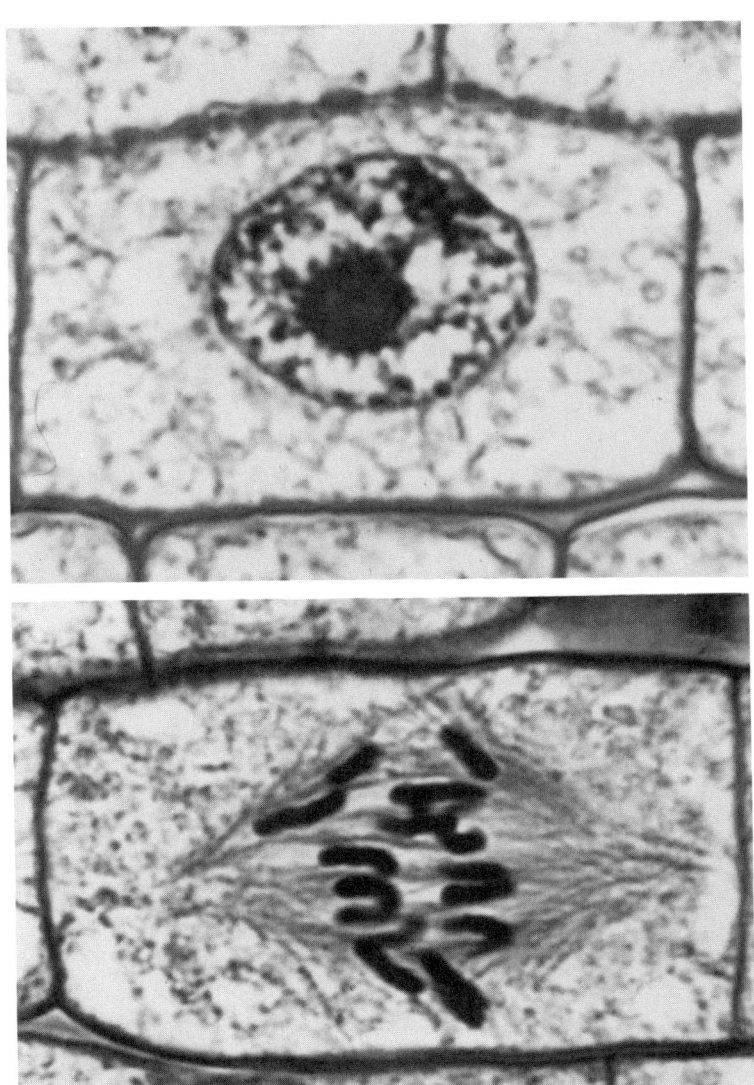

Top: *onion root tip cell.* Bottom: *onion root tip cell during mitosis. The dark "worms" are the chromosomes.*

mal to animal and plant to plant. Its composition may even change within different cells of the same organism.

All cytoplasm, however, contains certain compounds, all of which are made up of atoms of at least carbon, hydrogen, and oxygen. Sugars are some of the most important of these compounds. When we think of sugar, we normally think of ordinary table sugar, but there are actually hundreds of different sugars. For cells, the most important one is glucose, which acts like coal or oil in a furnace. When a cell needs fuel, it uses up or manufactures glucose.

The bricks and mortar, the nails and boards of the cell are **proteins.** Proteins are long, complex twisted molecules, built from smaller units called **amino acids.** Each amino acid contains not only carbon, hydrogen, and oxygen, but also nitrogen. Some proteins may run thousands of amino acids long and thus contain hundreds of thousands of carbon atoms, as opposed to glucose, which has only six carbon atoms.

Proteins, however, are more than just the structural material of the cell. As **enzymes,** some proteins ensure that all the necessary chemical reactions of the cell occur. As we shall see in the next chapter, the absence of even one of these enzymes can have tragic effects not only on the cell but also on the organism.

Naturally, something has to control the use of glucose, the manufacture of proteins, and the use of enzymes, as well as the maintenance and reproduction of the cell. And that something is a group of chemicals called **nucleic acids.** There are two types of nucleic acids: **DNA** (deoxyribonucleic acid) and **RNA** (ribonucleic acid). Found in the chromosomes, a mixture of DNA and proteins, DNA contains the genetic information that controls all activities in the cell, much like the dispatcher of a cab company determines where and when the drivers go to pick up a fare. The RNA carries that DNA information from the nucleus into the rest of the cell, just as radio waves carry dispatcher's instructions to the drivers.

PROBING THE CENTER

According to an old joke, a chicken is an egg's way of making another egg. Similarly, a cell is the DNA's way of making more DNA. The nucleic acids, DNA and RNA, are important, for without them, life as we know it would be impossible.

What makes DNA so important?

Of all chemical substances, it and RNA are the only ones that duplicate themselves—this is the basis of reproduction. And reproduction is one of the most basic characteristics of living organisms. There is not a species of single-celled organisms, nor of multicelled plants or animals, that cannot reproduce.

On a different level, DNA is the basis for heredity: the passing of physical and mental characteristics from parents to children. In the last quarter of a century, the study of heredity—called **genetics**—has increasingly become the study of DNA and its operation.

Early in the century, biologists recognized that heredity was controlled by genes. For most of this century, geneticists attempted to work out the mathematical patterns of inherited characteristics. Unfortunately, this method was of limited use since, even in a single-celled creature, there are thousands of traits with which to contend.

In 1953 came one of the great breakthroughs in biology, the revelation of DNA's role in heredity. James D. Watson, Sir Francis Crick, and Maurice Wilkins won a Nobel Prize for their work that revealed the famous double-helix structure of DNA and put forward the initial explanation of how DNA worked. Without their work, none of the advances in molecular biology seen today would be possible. Whoever controls a cell's genes, controls its molecular activity, and to control molecular activity is to control life.

The DNA molecule forms a double helix. The thread of a screw is a single helix, so imagine two such threads paralleling each other and you have a double helix (see Figure 2).

These threads or spirals—made up of carbon, oxygen, hydrogen, and phosphorus—are the twin backbones of the DNA molecule. Extending from each spiral at regular intervals are compounds called **nitrogen bases**. These nitrogen bases are nitrogen compounds, and in DNA there are four of them: adenine, thymine, guanine, and cytosine. Each links together with a matching nitrogen base or complementary nitrogen base from the other DNA spiral; adenine always links with thymine and cytosine with guanine. Thus, the mol-

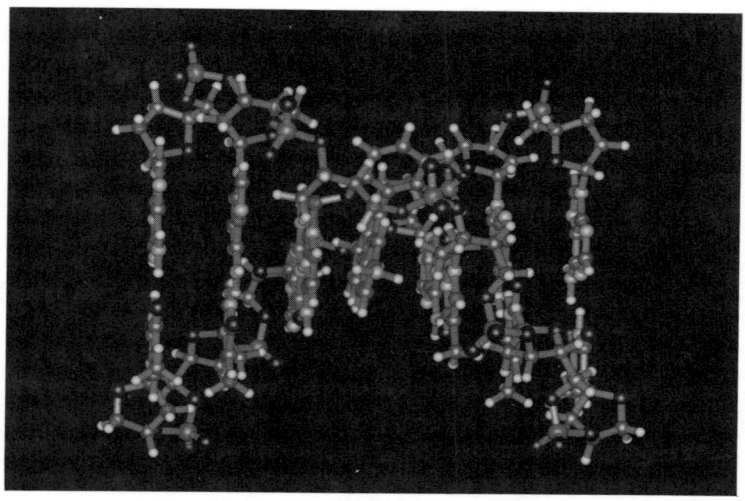

Computer-generated image of DNA molecule

ecule looks something like a spiral staircase, where each linked pair of nitrogen bases—adenine-thymine and cytosine-guanine—forms a step. Each DNA molecule consists of many units called nucleotides. These are made of the spiral backbone and a nitrogen base.

A DNA molecule can easily make a duplicate of itself—reproduce itself (see Figure 3). Each nucleotide separates from its partner, thus splitting the DNA molecule down the middle, much like opening a zipper on a jacket. Then each half of the spiral pulls in the material needed to reconstruct its partner thread. The final result: two molecules of DNA exactly like the original one.

TO MAKE A PROTEIN

Reproduction, however, is only one function of DNA. Indeed, most of DNA's work involves keeping the cell running, and biochemists—scientists who study the chemical nature of life—have a good idea how this nucleic acid does its work.

—22

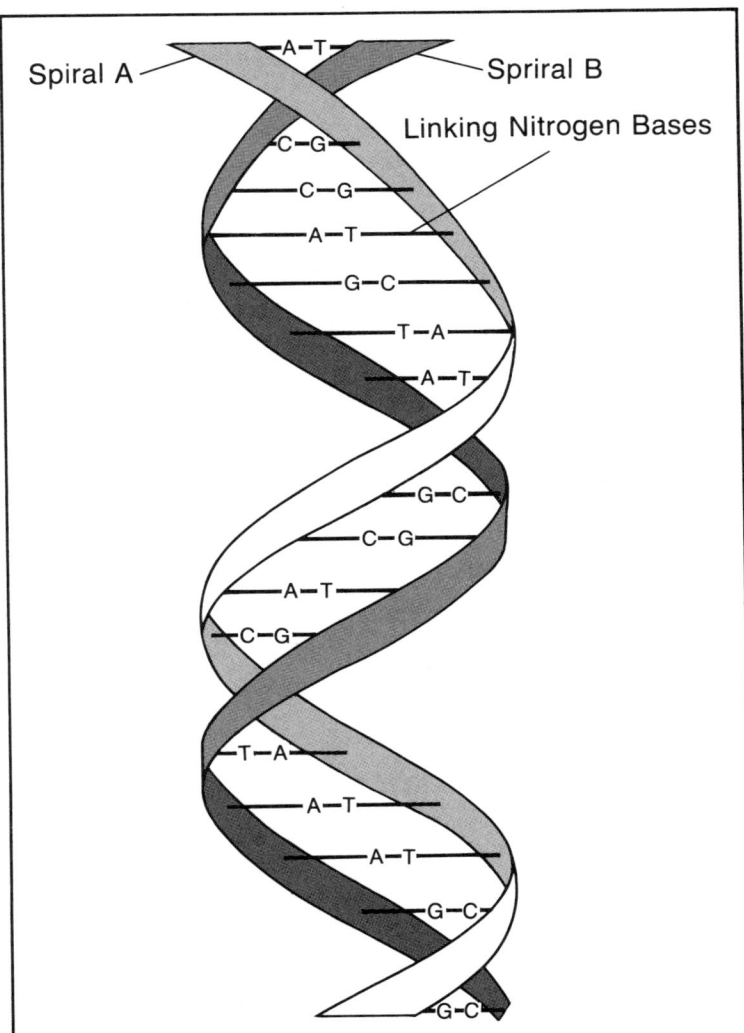

Figure 2. A representation of the double-helix structure of the DNA molecule. Linking the two spirals of the DNA are nitrogen bases: adenine (A), thymine (T), guanine (G), and cytosine (C).

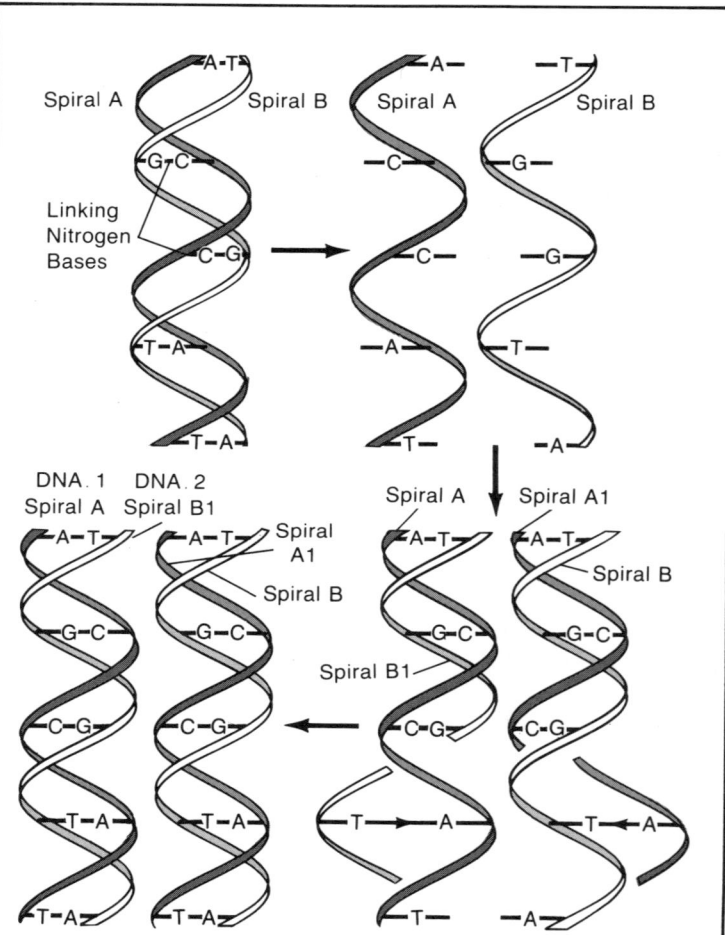

Figure 3. When a DNA molecule reproduces itself, its double helix splits down the middle, separating the two spirals into individual strands. The nitrogen bases—adenine (A), thymine (T), guanine (G), and cytosine (C)—on each strand fasten onto free counterparts and eventually reconstruct the other half of the helix. At the end of the process, there are two DNA double helixes, each an exact duplicate of the other.

Billions of nucleotides make up the DNA of any organism. These nucleotides form units that average a thousand nucleotides apiece. Each of these are the genes, and each one controls the production of one or more proteins. At one time, biological researchers thought that each gene produced one protein, but recent work shows that this is not the case. Thus, the several million genes may control the manufacture of several billion protein molecules.

At this point, we need to look at that other nucleic acid, RNA, because it plays a crucial role in this protein manufacturing. Although having a similiar chemical composition to DNA, RNA does not have the double-helix structure. Rather, its backbone is a single strand, off of which project the nitrogen bases (these are the same as those in DNA except for thymine, which in RNA is replaced by uracil).

Protein manufacturing (see Figure 4) begins in the cell when a special enzyme unzips a particular section of DNA—the gene in question—and breaks the links between the nucleotides. Instead of building from free-floating nucleotides more DNA, the unzipped section constructs an RNA molecule. This RNA, called **messenger RNA,** moves to the

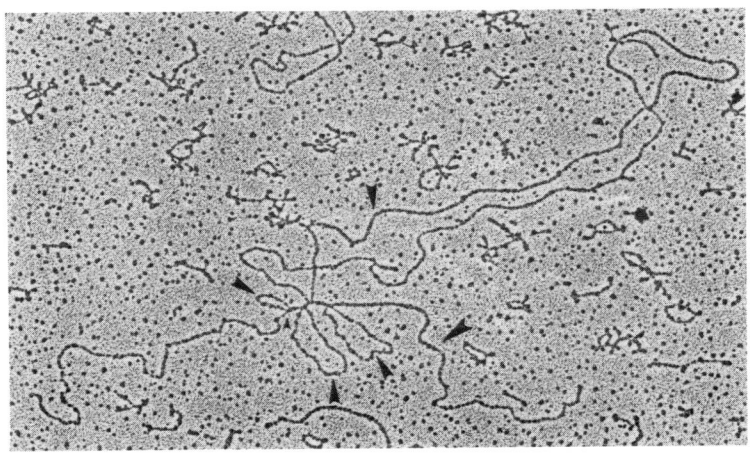

Photomicrograph of messenger RNA. The various arrows point to different parts of the messenger RNA.

—25

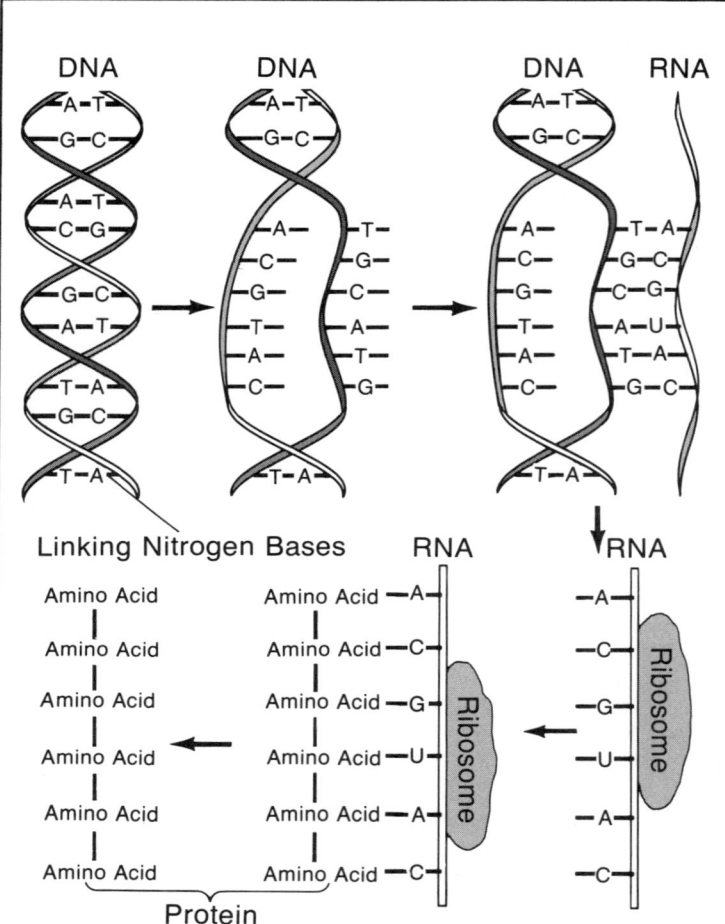

Figure 4. In protein production, part of a DNA double helix unzips, exposing the nitrogen bases: adenine (A), thymine (T), guanine (G), and cytosine (C). These nitrogen bases build an RNA molecule from free nitrogen bases [in RNA, uracil (U) replaces thymine]. The RNA carries the genetic message to a ribosome, where by pulling together various amino acids, it constructs the coded-for protein. The other of the nitrogen bases determines the arrangement of the amino acids and thus the protein's structure.

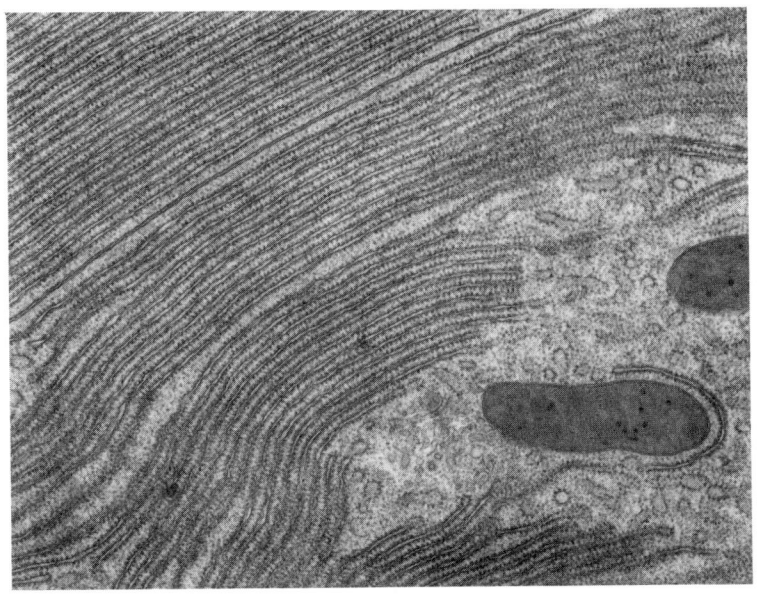

The small black dots in the "furrows" are ribosomes, the cell's protein factories.

protein factories of the cells, bodies called ribosomes (see Figure 1). Upon reaching a ribosome, the messenger RNA fastens to it, and the ribosome-RNA begins pulling amino acids together to form the specific protein coded for by the gene.

But how does the ribosome-RNA know which amino acids to add and in what order?

There is a code, the **genetic code.** Every three nucleotides of the messenger RNA stand for one amino acid. Say the RNA begins with the sequence adenine-uracil-guanine. This is the code for protein production to start with the amino acid methionine. Guanine-guanine-uracil calls for the addition of glycine. And so it goes until the protein is finished.

The genetic code has sixty-four possible "words." By the late 1960s, biochemists had deciphered the code and knew which triplets controlled which amino acids.

MORE REVELATIONS

The DNA model that Watson and Crick worked out in 1953, and the mechanisms for this molecule's operation, has an appealing completeness about it. It explains many things so well, but unfortunately it does not explain everything. As DNA research has progressed, particularly in the last decade, biochemists have discovered more about this molecule, and they are revolutionizing our ideas about DNA and the operation of genes.

No one has reason to question the basic double-helix structure of DNA, but recently MIT's Alexander Rich discovered that not all DNA is a smooth, spiraling helix. He found what he calls zigzag-DNA, or **Z-DNA.** In this DNA molecule, some of the nucleotide pairs stick out at an angle from the DNA spiral so that the structure looks as if it is zigzagging back and forth.

Rich thinks that this Z-DNA helps to regulate genetic activity by helping to determine what proteins will be manufactured and when. Genes are turned on and off by the fastening of various enzymes to specific nucleotide sites, and the Z-DNA may allow nucleotides that would normally be hidden from these enzymes to be exposed to these protein switches.

Rich also feels that Z-DNA may be involved in cancer. The exposed nucleotides are perhaps more vulnerable to attack by various carcinogenic chemicals than those hidden in the standard smooth DNA helix.

THE OTHER DNA

Although most of the DNA in a cell is in its nucleus, there is a small amount found in a series of cell bodies called **mitochondria.** These oval or worm-shaped structures provide energy to the cell through chemical reactions, many of which depend upon the sugar glucose. Recently, both they and their DNA have provoked some interesting speculation about their origins.

The DNA of the mitochondria differs from that found in the nucleus since it is nothing more than a naked double helix

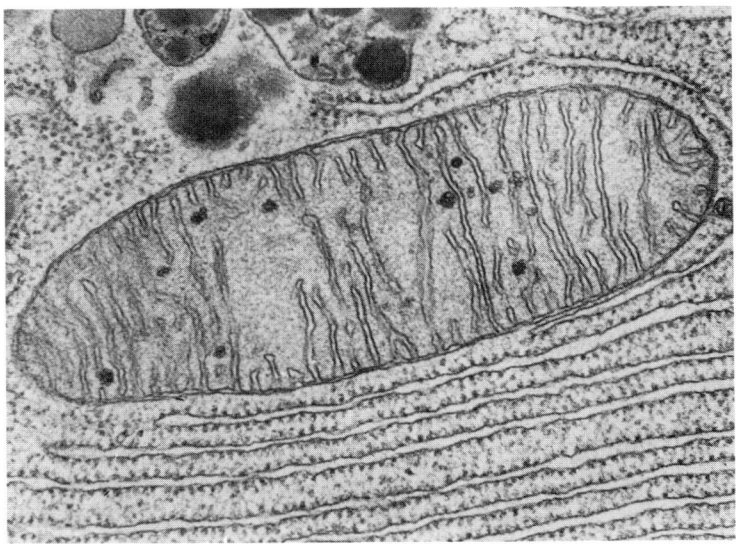

The mitochondrion provides energy for the cell through chemical reactions.

of nucleic acid. No protein is associated with it. In this absence of protein, this cellular DNA is very similar to that found in bacteria, a fact that recently has led some researchers, such as microbiologist Lynn Margulis of Boston University, to theorize that mitochondria originally were separate, individual cells.

Margulis and others feel that, in the early days of life on this planet, most one-celled organisms had difficulty in surviving the harsh conditions, particularly in utilizing oxygen to provide energy for themselves. According to theory, the mitochondrial ancestor would have been better at using oxygen in the environment. At some time, then, some of these pre-mitochondria were engulfed by another cell. The second cell would have benefited from the more efficient oxygen use of the engulfed organisms. Eventually, the pre-mitochondria would have become a permanent part of that predator cell,

—29

losing all its capabilities except its ability to provide energy. Indeed, Margulis feels that this happened many times with other types of organisms, accounting for the large number and complexity of the various structures in the modern cell.

What does "mitochondrial DNA" do? In contrast to nuclear DNA, seemingly very little actually. It does not control the production of proteins for building or maintaining cellular structures, not even its own. Nor does it help construct enzymes for general chemical reactions in the cell. Rather, it oversees the manufacture of the few enzymes it needs for its energy-producing reactions.

In 1981, B. G. Barrell of Cambridge University in Great Britain analyzed the nucleotide sequence of human mitochondrial DNA. Unsurprisingly, he found it composed of the expected DNA nucleotides—some fifteen thousand of them.

His other discovery, however, was not only surprising, it was startling. Mitochondrial DNA has a different genetic code from nuclear DNA. Where the triplet sequence adenine-guanine-adenine in nuclear DNA means add the amino acid arginine to a growing protein, in mitochondrial DNA it means stop protein production. This was the first evidence that the genetic code was not universal. It was also another piece of evidence that the mitochondria and the rest of the cell may well have arisen from separate organisms. If so, the mitochondrial ancestors had a different genetic code from those organisms that gave rise to the DNA found in the nucleus.

WHY THE DIFFERENCE?

Our body, like that of any multicellular organism, is made up of millions of cells, and every one of these cells has the exact same DNA. The DNA in one of our muscle cells has the same number and sequence of nucleotides as a cell in our brain, our heart, or our blood. Yet all of these cells perform different operations.

What causes this differentiation? No one knows. It is one of the great biological mysteries and one of the most important. If we could understand what caused one cell to work in the lungs and another to work in the small intestine, we would be well on the way to figuring out how to replace damaged cells or even whole organs.

Within the last few years, one possible explanation of cell differentiation has come into vogue. The cell's chromosomes are, as we saw earlier, a mixture of protein and DNA. The protein provides a spindle around which the DNA thread is wound.

Chromosomes themselves are coiled and folded in order to accommodate their lengths in the small volume of the nucleus. (When unfolded, the average human chromosome measures 6 feet, or about 2 meters, in length.) Quite possibly, then, each chromosome is folded differently depending upon whether its nucleus belongs to a muscle cell, a nerve cell, a liver cell, and so on. Different folds might expose different genes to the enzymes that activate genetic activity. The result could well affect protein production in the cell and consequently the nature of the cell.

INTO THE FACTORY

Now we have a general sense of the layout of the factory and what it can do. To control the cell factory, one need only control its genes. A much simpler thing to say than do. Indeed, until the early 1970s, such control was beyond even the most sophisticated biochemist, and although even partial control of the simplest cell is still a distant dream, biological scientists have begun working with actual DNA to make products and to gain further insights into the working of organisms. Let us now look at this greatest of all recent biological revolutions: genetic engineering.

CHAPTER 3
UNCOILING THE DOUBLE HELIX

THE EXPLOSIVE GENES

In the latter half of the twentieth century, and particularly in the last decade, genetic research has exploded into a frenzy of discovery. To give you some idea of the speed of this research, consider this: by 1971, researchers had mapped only three human genes out of an estimated one hundred thousand. By 1982, that number was over four hundred, and only three years later—1985—that number had more than quadrupled to seventeen hundred.

Accompanying this research explosion is an equally rapid progress in genetic manipulation or genetic engineering, the purposeful alteration of genes in microorganisms, plants, and animals. The results have been new medical and agricultural possibilities and a revolution unprecedented in the history of biology. In 1982, the federal Food and Drug Administration approved human insulin, produced by genetically altered bacteria, and at present, researchers have developed and are continuing to develop ways to test human genes for various diseases such as sickle-cell anemia and phenylketonuria. Other biological scientists have developed bacteria to decrease frost damage in crops. Such manipulation is at the heart and core of the modern **biotechnology**.

Biotechnology is the use of living creatures as well as natural or synthesized DNA, RNA, or proteins to manufacture new drugs, to create new medical procedures, to improve agricultural production; it is basically a living forge out of which a new industry is emerging. There has always been biological industry: for example, the fermentation that produces vinegar, wine, and beer is a biotechnological process. But as a major industrial force, biotechnology is a product of the last decade, with the most intensive biotechnological efforts today lying in the realm of genetic engineering.

To control specific genes is ultimately to control the production of specific proteins. It might at first seem simpler to find the protein one wanted to manufacture, figure out its structure, and manufacture it rather than fool around with genes. Proteins, however, are very complicated structures, often so twisted and convoluted in shape as almost to defy chemical analysis of their amino acid sequences and arrangements. It is actually chemically easier to deal with the less complicated structure and nucleotide sequence of the DNA's double helix. With DNA, a biochemist works with only four nucleotides, as opposed to the twenty amino acids that make up proteins.

Ultimately, the genetic revolution of the last decade and a half has converted biology from a primarily descriptive science to an active science. Biologists now find themselves able to alter and affect the organisms they could only study and describe a few years back. They are also faced with the same dilemma chemists found at the turn of the century: how to reconcile the need for honest scientific work and the increasing pressure from industry to create new valuable products for the marketplace. The scientific revolution has quickly turned into an industrial revolution, but it is too soon yet to know how biologists will handle themselves in their new commercial roles. We can only hope for the best.

CUT AND PASTE

The history of genetic engineering is short, going back only to the early 1970s when two scientists, Stanley Cohen of Stanford and Herbert Boyer of the University of California at San Francisco, actually inserted recombined DNA into *Escherichia coli* (*E. coli*) bacteria. To their delight, they found that the offspring of the bacteria carried exact copies of the foreign DNA.

As with all bacteria, *E. coli* has a single, circular chromosome that is made up exclusively of DNA. In addition to this central coil of DNA, each *E. coli* also has a scattering of very small DNA rings called plasmids.

After removing these plasmids, the biotechnician cuts them with an enzyme (see Figure 5). The cutting is quite accurate since the enzyme acts only on a specific nucleotide sequence. One early enzyme cut the DNA between guanine and adenine, but only when this combination appeared in the sequence guanine-adenine-adenine-thymine-thymine-cytosine.

DNA-cutting enzymes also leave the DNA segments with "sticky" ends: a short segment of DNA sticks out from the rest. These projecting single strands can bond to any other DNA segment with a complementary end.

Into the cut plasmid, then, the genetic engineer inserts another DNA segment (such as that which controls insulin production in humans) and reinserts the altered plasmid into *E. coli*. It takes only a short time—*E. coli* produce a new generation every twenty minutes—for a large number of bacteria to begin producing large quantities of insulin protein.

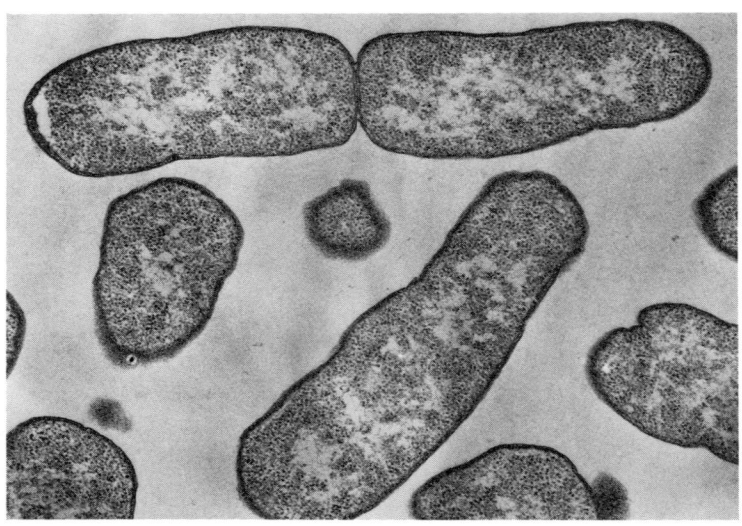

E. coli *bacteria are used in many experiments.*

—34

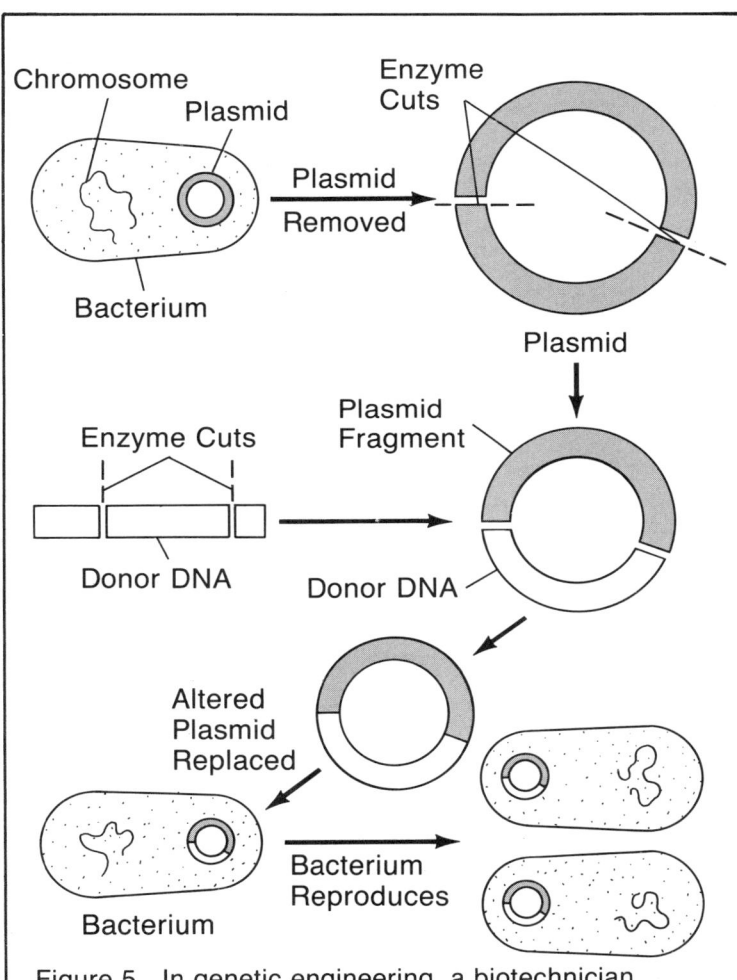

Figure 5. In genetic engineering, a biotechnician removes a bacterial DNA segment, called a plasmid, and using enzymes, cuts away part of it. The technician then cuts the donor DNA from another gene, and with another enzyme, fuses it together with the plasmid fragment. The new combined DNA is inserted into a bacterium, which reproduces the altered plasmid as it breeds.

You might wonder why bacteria are used instead of human cells that produce human biochemicals. The technique for cultivating human cells has been available since the early part of this century, and cultures of such cells were used to grow polio viruses used to make a polio vaccine.

Human cells, however, are more difficult to grow than are microorganisms. First, the nutritional requirements are much more complicated for human cell cultures than bacterial cultures. Second, the temperature is very critical for human cells. Two degrees plus or minus, and the cells can die. Third, human cells are slow to reproduce, taking twenty-four hours to grow a new generation. Compare that to the twenty to sixty minutes needed to produce a generation of bacteria.

HAZARDS

As with most major scientific breakthroughs, genetic engineering offers not only benefits but risks. Indeed, from the beginning of this work, both scientists and nonscientists have called for strict regulation and extreme caution.

Because so much of present genetic engineering involves the use of microorganisms, critics have a legitimate concern about the possible consequences to the general environment if such organisms escaped from labs or test areas. This possible danger does not generally come from the inserted genetic material, but from **mutations,** further changes in this altered DNA caused by background radiation, mistakes in DNA duplication, or chemical agents. Such mutations might prove deadly to both animals and plants.

A rapid spread of genetically altered and mutated bacteria of one species could be bad enough, but other species of microorganisms might soon be carrying this altered DNA. In 1985, Stuart B. Levy of Tufts University School of Medicine reported that bacteria of many species exchange plasmids, so that if a genetically altered species invaded a bacterial community, its engineered DNA could eventually find its way into most of the other species' DNA.

Because of such fears and such findings, genetic engineers do most of their initial work using a strain of *E. coli* that cannot live outside special laboratory conditions. Further, both the Environmental Protection Agency (EPA) and the U.S. Department of Agriculture (USDA) have regulatory committees designed to oversee actual field experiments of genetically altered microorganisms.

Critics such as Jeremy Rifkin of the Foundation on Economic Trends, however, feel that neither regulatory committee is very effective. Indeed, Rifkin has filed several law suits blocking field tests of genetically altered microorganisms by firms such as Advanced Genetic Sciences, Inc., of Oakland, California, and Agracetus of Middleton, Wisconsin, even though these tests were approved by the EPA.

Nor is Rifkin the only one concerned about the ability of these committees to oversee such experiments. Over the past two years, a U.S. Senate committee has held hearings on this matter. The goal of these hearings is to determine how effective present regulation is and how a national set of controls could be applied to genetic engineering research.

And there does seem to be a need for such questioning. In early 1986, the USDA admitted it not only had fieldtested a genetically engineered vaccine for pseudo-rabies, a deadly killer of pigs, but had also authorized TechAmerica Group, Inc., of Omaha, Nebraska, to sell it. And its regulatory committee? The USDA had not even consulted it. This admission did nothing to ease fears of the ineffectiveness of such regulation. Society has a right to be protected from dangers posed by scientific research, and certainly humans have been responsible for enough ecological damage to this planet. Thus, few scientists would argue against the need for effectively regulating genetic engineering. Most, however, feel that this genetic work offers too many medical and agricultural benefits to be stopped—the goal of some critics of DNA manipulation. As with all scientific advances, researchers must seek ways of decreasing, if not eliminating, the risks, while maintaining a steady pace of discovery.

OFF THE
ASSEMBLY LINE

To date, medicine is the field that has most profited from the new genetic research, for genetic engineering is creating

A tank for processing amino acids and proteins at a plant owned by the Genex Corporation, a biotechnology company

new and revolutionary medical procedures. The California biotechnical firm Genentech, under contract to Eli Lilly and Company, has successfully inserted the gene that controls the manufacture of human **insulin** into bacterial plasmids and has produced large quantities of this material. Without insulin, the human body cannot use glucose very well, and diabetics, those people whose bodies do not make this substance, eventually weaken and die.

Insulin, of course, has been available to diabetics for decades, but this is not human insulin. Rather, it is insulin extracted from pigs or cattle; it is neither practical nor economical to obtain human insulin. Although far better than nothing, swine or bovine insulin does not work as well as actual human insulin, and insulin is structurally too complicated to synthesize in commercial amounts. So, the news that genetically engineered bacteria are capable of producing true human insulin in large enough quantities for diabetics to use is welcome news.

CREATING THE MIRACLE

Insulin is not the only substance being manufactured by genetically engineered bacteria. Interferon is a chemical produced naturally by the body that appears effective against many infectious diseases. Indeed, doctors are hoping that interferon may eventually prove to be a miracle drug for the cure of many types of **cancers.** Cancers are wild, uncontrolled growths of cells.

Working with interferon in the past was both difficult and costly: to treat one patient took $20,000 to $30,000 of this drug because the body produces it only in small amounts. But by inserting the proper genetic fragment into a bacterial plasmid and growing it, biotechnicians are now able to provide medical research with as much human interferon as necessary.

In 1985, using such bacterially produced interferon, Gilbert Jay of the National Cancer Institute reported that he had discovered what this substance does to cancer cells. The human body, as with all organisms, has a system for fighting disease and infection. This system, however, does not respond to cancer cells, and Jay showed that the source of this failure is the absence of certain proteins on the surfaces of cancer cells. Interferon, however, apparently stimulates this protein to appear on the surfaces of these cells, and when the protein does, the body's defenses attack and kill the malignant cells.

When Jay injected specific interferon-treated cancer cells into lab animals, he found they became immune to that particular cancer. He is hoping eventually to prepare a similar treatment for humans against at least some cancers.

GENES GONE WRONG

But the answer to the problem of cancer may also lie in direct analysis and treatment of human genes. In the early 1970s, researchers discovered that some cancers were directly linked to specific genes. These cancer-producing genes are already present in human chromosomes. Indeed, normally, these genes seem to play an important role in cell reproduction and differentiation—remember that a cancer is an uncontrolled growth of cells.

The search is now on for the mechanism that triggers these normally harmless genes into deadly killers. Doctors hope that by finding these causes, they will learn to control these cancer genes. This genetic research is a medical revolution in the making since, if the researchers gain control of these genes, they will have brought to bay one of the greatest killers in human history.

In search of this goal, Robert Weinberg of MIT has shown that, in human bladder cancer, the trigger is a mutation of one of these genes. The source of such mutations can be radiation, a cancer-causing chemical, or a **virus**—a very small microorganism that has RNA for its genetic core and that uses other cells' genetic material for reproduction.

Another way in which these cancer genes become active is when they hop from one chromosome to another. In this way, the transplanted gene interferes with the normal activity of its new chromosomal home, and the result can be uncontrolled cellular reproduction and growth.

Scientists such as Philip Leder of Harvard Medical School have recently discovered that when these cancer genes become active, they often begin producing specific proteins. With this knowledge, doctors should be able to design tests to check whether individual cells have suddenly begun manufacturing these particular protein clues. If so, they will then know that one or more of these cancer genes is active and thus be able to detect the onset of cancer much earlier than they can at present.

Of course, the eventual goal is the design and use of drugs that would specifically turn off these genes. If that can be done, it would be far superior to the present anti-cancer drugs, which not only kill cancer cells but also normal, healthy cells.

GENE DIAGNOSIS

Cancer is not the only disease arising from a genetic flaw or failure. There are over three thousand such human diseases, many of which remain hidden in the genetic complexity of the cell until they suddenly appear to claim another victim. But, researchers have begun working out genetic tests to detect some of these afflictions so that, where possible, preventive steps may be taken.

At Johns Hopkins School of Medicine, Corinne D. Boehm and a research team have developed such a genetic test to detect sickle-cell anemia in children before birth. Sickle-cell anemia is a hereditary disease that causes the oxygen-carrying red blood cells to alter shape; in so doing, they often clog blood vessels and interfere with blood circulation. This genetic disease kills twelve hundred to eighteen hundred newborns a year; it may also appear much later in an individual's life and is almost always fatal.

Prior to Boehm's work, the only way of testing a pre-born baby for this disease was to draw a blood sample from it, a process that was fatal 3 percent of the time. Boehm's test, however, relies on the use of DNA found floating in the fluid surrounding the baby in the mother's womb. With this DNA, a doctor is able to determine whether the baby is carrying the sickle-cell anemia gene, even before the baby is born.

Such genetic diagnosis is accomplished in at least two ways. First, the doctor can use a DNA-cutting enzyme, much like those used to cut bacterial plasmids. The enzyme cuts the healthy gene at a specific adenine nucleotide. In the sickle-cell gene, thymine replaces this adenine. This single substitution means that this disorder arises because one human protein differs from another by only a single amino acid. The biochemical health of any organism often depends upon a precarious balance.

The doctor testing for sickle-cell anemia then cuts the DNA sample with an enzyme. If it is a healthy gene, then he or she obtains a short DNA fragment. However, if it is a sickle-cell gene, the enzyme will not be able to cut at the same point, and the result will be a much longer DNA fragment.

The second genetic test method requires the use of a DNA probe. Such a probe is a short length of DNA whose nucleotide sequence complements a specific section of the faulty gene. The sickle-cell gene has one segment that is cytosine-cytosine-thymine-guanine-thymine. A DNA probe for this gene would have a sequence guanine-guanine-adenine-cytosine-adenine. Being complements, the two sequences would eventually bind together into the double-helix structure.

For purposes of detection, the probe contains a radioactive carbon or nitrogen atom. After the probe is introduced to the suspect gene, it is given time to bind. Then the researcher cuts up the DNA with enzymes. If the gene is defective, one of these fragments will be radioactive from the bound DNA probe. If, however, it is not a sickle-cell gene, the probe will not have bound, and none of the fragments will show any radioactivity. The diagnosis would show normal genetic material.

TOO BIG

The actual location of any genetic flaw can be relatively confined as with sickle-cell anemia's single nucleotide switch, or it can be complicated. Indeed, in some diseases, such as **PKU** (phenylketonuria), it can involve variations in nonactive regions of the gene.

PKU victims are missing an enzyme needed to break down phenylalanine, a chemical whose toxic effects lead to mental retardation. PKU victims can be aided by a special diet, and for some years now, hospitals have been applying a test for PKU among newborn babies. Some researchers, however, feel that a genetic test of preborn infants would be even more effective in detecting and handling this disorder. And L. C. Woo of Baylor College of Medicine in Houston has the beginnings of such a test.

The gene whose damage results in PKU is made up mostly of long segments that have no apparent function. Biologists have discovered that, although the same gene will have the same primary information on it, it will also have sections that differ from person to person. In most cases, these differences have no effect upon proper functioning of the gene.

For some years now, biologists have known that genes are made up of segments, among which—at the beginning and end of the gene—are sections to stop and start messenger RNA production (see Figure 6). In the early 1980s,

—42

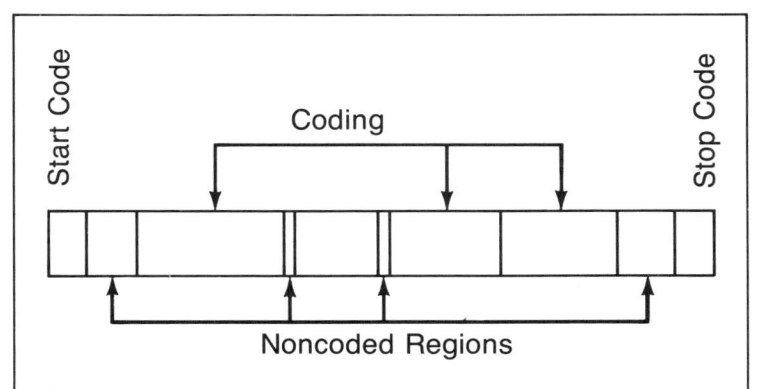

Figure 6. A gene has several sections. At the beginning is a section coded to start the formation of an RNA molecule. The actual information for protein production—transferred to the manufactured RNA—is in the coded sections, which are often separated by noncoded sections. The final segment ends the RNA formation.

researchers discovered that many genes also had nonfunctional or noncoded areas (see Figure 6). When the messenger RNA is manufactured, these units are also reproduced, but are later cut out before the RNA moves to the ribosome.

But, according to Woo, the gene that controls production of the phenylalanine enzyme has an astonishingly large number of these noncoded regions. Only 3 percent of its length is involved with manufacturing the crucial enzyme. The rest apparently does nothing. Unfortunately, because of its very length, variations in these noncoded regions are possible, and while most are harmless, Woo and his colleagues have found four that are not. These four alterations account for some 90 percent of PKU cases. At present, Woo is able to identify preborn infants who possess one of these flaws, and he hopes soon to be able to identify the others.

But Woo's eventual goal, as it is with many researchers, is an actual genetic cure for genetic disorders such as PKU. Woo has already produced a human genetic fragment that eliminates the troublesome phenylalanine-enzyme's gene section. Using a virus, he has successfully inserted this fragment into lab-grown cells and produced the needed enzyme.

GENE THERAPY

Woo's proposed genetic cure of PKU is an example of gene therapy. Many doctors feel that this process will be one of the most revolutionary steps in medicine since it will eventually lead to the complete elimination of any disease with a genetic basis. At present, most of these three thousand genetic diseases either lack cures or have insufficient remedies. Now, for the first time in human history, the medical profession is actually looking at a practical and obtainable way of destroying these killers.

How close are doctors to trying actual gene therapy on human patients? Very close. In 1985, W. French Anderson of the National Institutes of Health announced he was ready to propose an experimental program of human gene therapy. Anderson, who has been working on a genetic cure for a disorder that renders sufferers prone to infectious diseases and an early death, feels confident in the worth and safety of his work. Whether it comes in the form of Anderson's work or another researcher's, gene therapy, along with all the other medical possibilities from genetic engineering, is a revolution whose time appears to have arrived.

And potential hazards notwithstanding, we are only at the beginning of the genetics revolution. Where it will take us, only time will tell, but the world it is creating will be as different from our present one as it is from the pre-Industrial Revolution world of the eighteenth century. We must hope we travel prudently and arrive safely.

CHAPTER 4
TAKING THE MEASURE OF LIFE

A scientific revolution needs tools if it is to move forward. In this respect, biology is no different from chemistry or physics. Granted, there is still progress in biological areas such as evolution, ecology, and sociobiology that is generated by observations made by the unaided human, but when we speak of cellular and molecular biology, we are in a realm in which the unaided human cannot function—cannot even see.

TO SEE THE INVISIBLE

Rising three stories high, drawing a million volts of power, and costing some $3 million, the New York Department of Health's **HVEM,** the high-voltage electron microscope, is probably the most expensive instrument ever devised for biological investigation. Yet, with the three of these in the United States, researchers have been able to look closely at the structure of chromosomes, watch specific parts of a reproducing cell's nucleus, and turn out three-dimensional images of complete cells.

If any one scientific tool symbolizes biology, it is the microscope. Since its invention in the seventeenth century, the microscope has allowed biologists to probe more and more deeply into the normally inaccessible regions of living things. They have contributed more to our understanding of life than any other single instrument.

Not surprisingly, the microscope in all its myriad modern guises is still centrally important to biology. It continues to provide information upon which many of the modern biological revolutions are built, and as with most of biology, it is undergoing its own series of revolutions.

THE CHANGING SCOPE

There are a wide variety of microscopes. Some—called simple microscopes—have a single lens (a magnifying glass is technically a microscope). Others, called compound microscopes, have two or more lenses. And still others, **electron microscopes** do not have glass lenses at all, but magnetic lenses.

A scanning transmission electron microscope at Brookhaven National Laboratory. The STEM works by illuminating a specimen with electronics, focusing the electrons onto a small spot on the specimen, and scanning the spot across the specimen. Signals from the specimen are then analyzed by computer to produce an image.

If the types of microscopes vary, so does the degree of magnification. Assuming that the magnification of our naked eyes is one, then a simple microscope can magnify up to six hundred times. With this, we can see some microorganisms and the details of body tissue. The compound microscope extends this magnification up to two thousand times over the human eye and is good enough to see inside animal and plant cells as well as bacteria. The electron microscope may be able to magnify things up to one million times. With it, we can see such minute structures as viruses and massive molecules.

In the electron microscope, instead of light being shined through the specimen, an electron beam passes through it. Electrons are the negatively charged particles that circle the nucleus of atoms. With a strong enough electric current, these electrons can be stripped away and projected in a beam. Such a projector is a cathode ray tube—very similar to the tube that forms the core of a TV set. In an electron microscope, the electron gun shoots its electron beam down between magnetic coils (see Figure 7). These coils act as lenses to focus and magnify. After the beam passes through the specimen, the final enlarged image is caught on photographic film or transmitted to a TV monitor.

Thus, the HVEM, first put into operation a little over a decade ago, is merely the successor of a long line of microscopes. It, however, has several advantages over earlier electron microscopes.

First, unlike the conventional electron microscope, the HVEM can provide images of whole cells and whole cellular structures such as mitochondria. With other electron microscopes, such specimens would be too thick, and the operator has to cut them into a series of thin slices. After obtaining images of all the slices, the researcher then would, using these images, try to build a picture of the whole object. Such a reconstruction can lead to errors because it depends upon a certain amount of guesswork as to the way in which the separate slices are connected. So the HVEM's complete image allows biologists for the first time to see how many of these cellular structures actually appear.

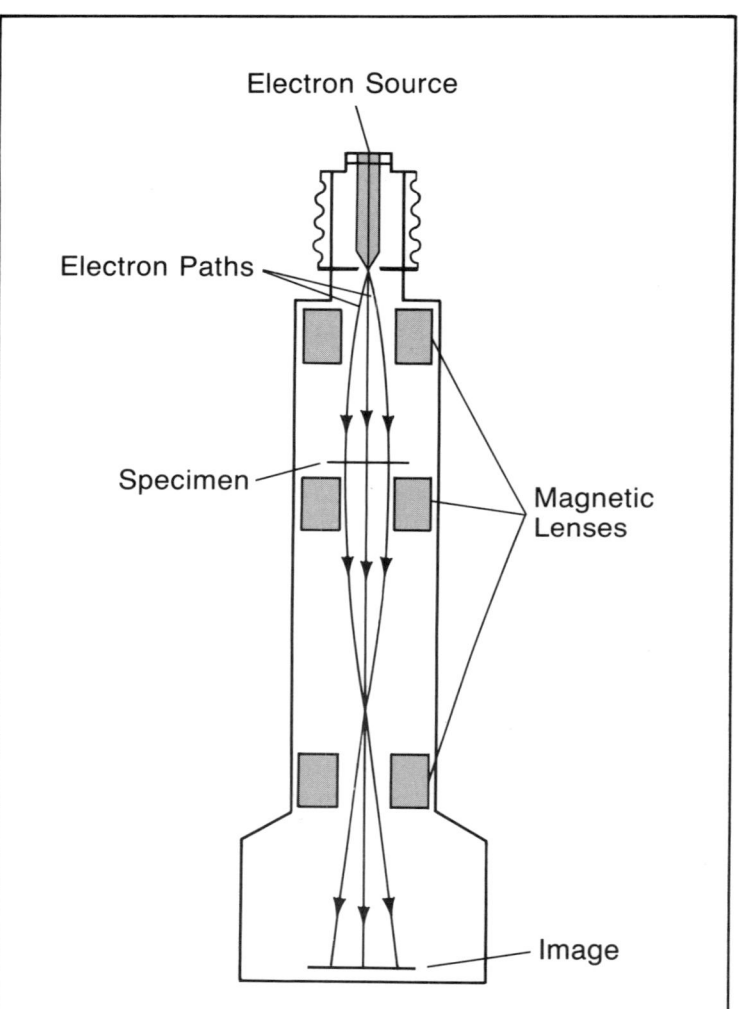

Figure 7. Diagram of an electron microscope. The electron source at the top sends out a beam of electrons, which are focused by magnetic lenses that form an image of the specimen on a photographic plate at the bottom of the microscope.

Second, and again unlike conventional electron microscopes, is the HVEM's ability to create three-dimensional images. Undoubtedly the most revolutionary aspect of the HVEM, this process is done very much as it would be in a 3-D movie. Two images of the object are made and then projected side by side. The biologist views the two images through special glasses that make the object appear to rise out of the TV monitor screen. To make viewing easier, a computer adds different colors to different structures. The computer can also rotate the object or cut through it to present a cross section of any part of the image. For the observer, it is as though he or she is actually watching a giant-sized cell or chromosome.

SEEING BY FEEL

But the HVEM is not the ultimate in microscopes. At present, that position is reserved for the **STM,** the Scanning Tunneling Microscope. Designed and built by Gerd Binnig and Heinrich Rohrer of IBM Zurich Research Laboratory, the STM is unique among microscopes since it has no lenses. Instead, a needle-like probe runs just above the surface of the specimen being observed. All objects are surrounded by a cloud of electrons, and the electron cloud of the probe's tip tracks across the electron cloud just above the specimen's surface. It is not unlike a phonograph needle riding along a record's groove. Where the phonograph needle reads the record's groove for information to be turned into sound, the STM's probe reads the contours of the specimen. This information is then fed into a computer, which creates a TV image.

The STM is extremely sensitive. E. Courtens of the IBM Zurich Research Laboratory has observed nucleotide sequences in DNA with it. Arthuro Baroa and his colleagues of the Autonomous University of Madrid have studied in detail the head of the phi 29 virus, whose dimensions are 0.0000008 inch (0.000002 centimeter) across. In fact, the STM is so sensitive that it can show individual atoms and molecules in substances, an important step in genetic and molecular engineering, where products are made by shifting such molecular units.

But the STM may have an even more direct role to play in genetic engineering than mere observation of DNA. Theoretically, the probe not only can see atoms and molecules in specimens but it can also be directed to pick them up and move them. In the not-too-distant future, it may be possible literally to take a protein or a nucleic acid and shuffle its components around to suit your needs. The ultimate result may be the manufacture of small biological "machines" that can troubleshoot our bodies. Such "machines" may be able to monitor the condition of all the cells in the body, providing needed proteins or other chemicals to those cells that either have lost the capability or never had the art of manufacturing their own. They may further be able to chase down and destroy invading cold viruses and even devour developing cancer cells.

IN THE PALM OF THE HAND

Despite the increasing advent of microscopes such as the HVEM and the STM, the light microscope still plays an important role in the biological sciences since great magnification is not always needed. Further, it is very easy for any biologist to have a compound microscope in his or her lab, whereas all electron microscopes require special housing and are not usually found in individual labs.

Not all research, however, can be done in a lab, and biologists doing fieldwork often need microscopes for their work. Since good compound microscopes are heavy, field biologists do not generally find them practical to carry around. But there is one, the MacArthur Portable, that can be held in one hand.

The whole unit fits easily in the palm of the hand. Mounted on a slide are three different power lenses that can be moved into place quickly and easily (see Figure 8). On top, at one end, a mirror directs light downward through a lens. After passing through the specimen, the light hits a right-angle prism, is shot across to another right-angle prism, and then up through the eyepiece.

And the portable does work, having been used all over

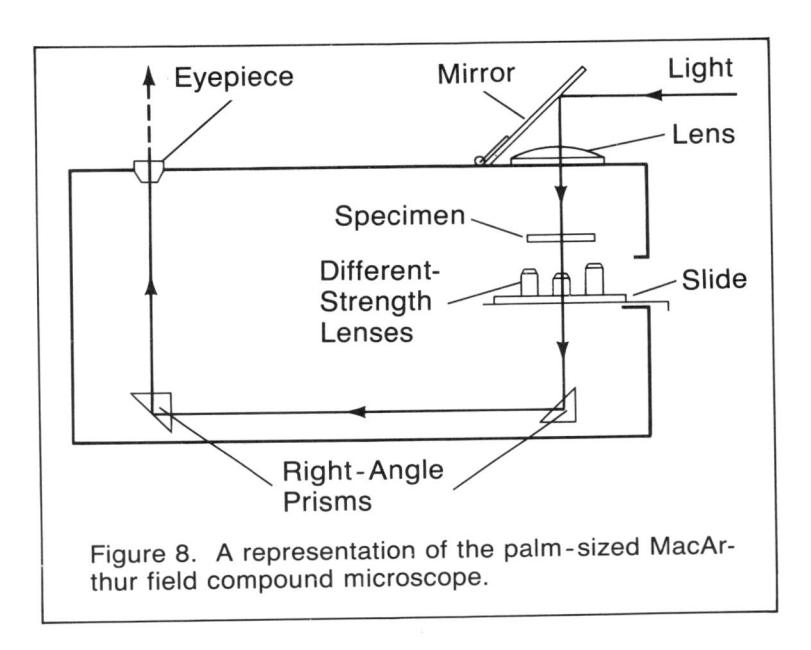

Figure 8. A representation of the palm-sized MacArthur field compound microscope.

the world in all kinds of conditions. It is also tough, for at least one of these portables has been run over by a truck and another dropped out of an airplane. Neither suffered any damage.

X-RAY VISION

At first, the image is nothing more than a black-and-white picture, looking like a particularly complicated architectural diagram of some sort of storage silo. Then colors begin appearing: yellow for most of the image, with brown to indicate shading. At the end, it looks like a very fat cornflake.

Is this some sort of new art form? No, it is a computer-generated and computer-colored image of the coated protein of a tobacco mosaic virus. Such work by Keiichi Namaba and Donald L. Caspar of the Structural Biological Laboratory of Brandeis University is the latest advance in using X rays to observe microscopic detail.

Computer-generated image of a tobacco mosaic virus

One of the advantages that X rays have over both light and electron beams is their ability to reveal details about the structure of molecules. Indeed, except for the STM—which is only now becoming operational in the mid-1980s—few other instruments will show such detail. Almost all knowledge of DNA and protein structure has come from X rays: Watson and Crick's 1953 revelation of DNA's double-helix structure was based on X-ray studies.

Until the recent work of Namaba and Caspar, the images with which researchers had to work were flat black-and-white representations. It was often difficult to tell much about such images, even with years of training. But by giving an illusion through color shading, the new computer-generated images aid the eye in discovering and tracing out structural patterns in molecules. This is only another step in the rapid progress of biochemistry that is giving researchers a better understanding of the nature of DNA and proteins.

So far, we have concentrated on the search for the very small—the secrets of the cell and the molecule. We shall see, however, that what cell biologists and biochemists have discovered through their research is likewise important to the revolutions going on in the other areas of the life sciences. As we shall see in the next chapter, the evidence for the various new ideas on evolutionary theory eventually lead to the genes and DNA. So the instruments to probe the very small also indirectly probe the very large.

CHAPTER 5
DISCOVERING THE WAYS OF CHANGE

The Galápagos Islands. Straddling the equator, these volcanic islands rise out of the Pacific Ocean some 650 miles (1,100 kilometers) west of Ecuador. For some three hundred years after their discovery by Spanish explorers, these islands provided a meeting ground for pirates, warships, and whaling vessels. But in 1835, they provided the stage from which one of the great revolutions in biology was launched.

Charles Darwin, a young geologist aboard the British exploration ship the *Beagle*, became very interested in the extreme diversity of the various animals and birds to be found on these isolated islands: he found fourteen species of finches alone. From his observations in the Galápagos and later in both South America and Australia, he eventually worked out a theory of evolution, which he presented to the world in 1859 in *On the Origin of Species by Means of Natural Selection*.

Species is the term biologists use to describe a population of plants or animals or microorganisms that not only share similar physical and biochemical characteristics but that can also interbreed. Ideally, individuals from two different species—chimpanzees and spider monkeys, for example—cannot have offspring. Species division does not always draw a firm line since horses and donkeys—two different species—can breed and produce mules. Mules, however, are not fertile and cannot produce other mules.

Evolution is the process by which organisms—over a period of time—change their physical and chemical natures and, in the process, create new species. Through evolution, the early simpler life forms on earth diversified into the more

Charles Darwin

Galápagos Islands in Ecuador

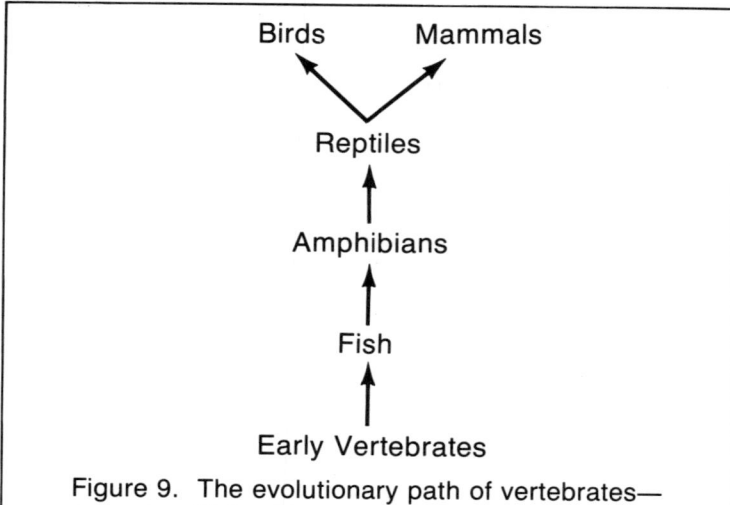

```
        Birds    Mammals
           ↖     ↗
          Reptiles
             ↑
          Amphibians
             ↑
            Fish
             ↑
       Early Vertebrates
```

Figure 9. The evolutionary path of vertebrates—animals with backbones.

complex forms of today. It was this evolutionary process that created the multitude of present-day species. Figure 9 shows the evolutionary pathway of the **vertebrates,** animals with backbones.

Appropriately, this theory of evolution that deals with the process of change and development in living things has undergone its own share of change in the last century and a quarter. And today it is changing once again. The original revolution continues to be revolutionized.

NATURAL SELECTION

Despite modifications, particularly with the discoveries of genes and then DNA, Darwin's theory of evolution through **natural selection** remains an important part of most biologists' concept about evolution. Natural selection is the process that favors the survival of individuals in a population, those who are best suited to cope with a particular environment. Such individuals will live longer than others who lack these traits. By living longer, these hardier specimens will

A flightless cormorant, a marine iguana, and a scarlet crab perched on a rock on one of the Galápagos Islands, off the coast of Ecuador, in South America. The extraordinary diversity of life on these islands helped inspire Darwin to conceive of the theory of evolution.

produce more offspring. Eventually, given enough time, every member of the population will possess these survival characteristics. Thus, those who are most fit to survive in any particular environment are chosen by natural selection to do so.

One of the most spectacular cases of natural selection in this century involved the peppered moth of Great Britain. Generally, these moths are a light gray, which blends well with the color of tree trunks in those areas where they live. Occasionally, however, a black moth would be born, and because it stood out in sharp contrast against the light-colored tree trunks, it was quickly eaten by birds. Natural selection favored the gray moth.

Times change and so do environments. The trees in some areas of the peppered moth's territory became blackened through industrial pollution. Suddenly, the original gray color became a liability, and birds began eating these lighter-colored moths and missing the darker black moths, whose coloration now acted as protective camouflage. The moth populations in these polluted areas quickly became black.

And what happened when British industries began installing pollution control devices? The trees in the affected areas became light again, and the environment once more favored the light gray moths. This is an example of natural selection at work.

A similar process would account for the fourteen finch species Darwin discovered on the Galápagos Islands. Only one or two founding species would have had to migrate some 1 or 2 million years ago from the mainland to the islands. Different environmental pressures on the individual islands would have favored finches with different beak shapes, developed to cope with different insects and different flowers, until the final result—fourteen distinct species of this one bird alone on these isolated islands.

MOLECULAR EVOLUTION

Darwinists see evolution as a constant ongoing process, and the changes that adapt an entire population to any environment gradually accumulate over many generations. In the twentieth century, biologists have linked this change to alteration in the genes. Indeed, it would be truer to say that natural selection favors specific genes or gene combinations rather than individuals in a population.

One way in which such genetic change occurs is through a recombination of existing genes. In 1985, Thomas Sudhof of the University of Texas Health Science Center at Dallas reported one way in which new genes are created from portions of preexisting genes. It is as though genes are made up of modules—discrete pieces that can be pulled out and rearranged in various combinations. Modern stereo equipment is modular. You can pull out the receiver, the speakers, the various tape disks, or the turntable from one system and plug them into a second system, making whatever combinations you want. The same, in a more complex fashion, seems to happen in the formation of some new genes that lead to successful environmental adaptations.

Sudhof studied the sequences of a human gene known to control the transport of cholesterol—a chemical associated with hardening of the arteries. He found that one section of the gene was exactly like a section of a gene involved in growth and that a second section paralleled a piece of another gene associated with human blood plasma production.

Besides recombining genes, evolutionary change arises from mutation, actual alterations in the genes caused by background radiation, mistakes in DNA duplication, and so on. On a molecular level, mutation means some change in an organism's DNA. That alteration may merely be the substitution of one pair of nucleotides, say, adenine-thymine, for another pair, say, guanine-cytosine. Or it may mean a change in a whole sequence of nucleotides.

The result in either case shows up in protein production, for the altered DNA will produce a new protein. Most such proteins will have little effect on the organism, but a few will provide some small benefit toward survival.

Because a change in some proteins in any organism may be fatal, particularly if it is a crucial enzyme, mutations often arise from duplication of genes. Thus, there will be through some accident in reproduction of the DNA molecule a nucleotide section manufactured twice. This means that one of the twin genes may still control the production of the original protein, while its duplicate may mutate and create a new protein that possibly may enhance survival.

A SUDDEN CHANGE

With all sciences, new knowledge requires that old knowledge be reexamined. This reexamination may mean that the old knowledge must be thrown away—discarded because it is now realized to be false. Such was the fate of the earth-centered universe idea when Copernicus's sun-centered solar system model was accepted in the sixteenth century. More often, however, the new knowledge complements the old. Thus, Einstein's relativistic physics did not overthrow Newtonian physics, but rather placed the latter in a new framework.

Evolutionary theory is no exception to this need of periodic reexamination. Within the last decade, many biologists have begun questioning whether natural selection is the only mechanism controlling evolution. Indeed, some, such as Stephen Jay Gould of the Museum of Comparative Zoology of Harvard University and Niles Eldredge of the American Museum of Natural History, wonder if the role of natural selection is not vastly overrated. If these critics of natural selection are correct, then they have significantly modified the theory of evolution.

As we have seen, Darwinists see evolution as a constant ongoing process in which adaptive changes from genetic recombinations or mutations accumulate slowly over many generations. Gould and Eldredge do not fault the mechanism of mutation and recombining genes as an explanation of evolutionary change. However, they do feel that such changes

Stephen Jay Gould believes that mechanisms other than natural selection play a significant role in evolution.

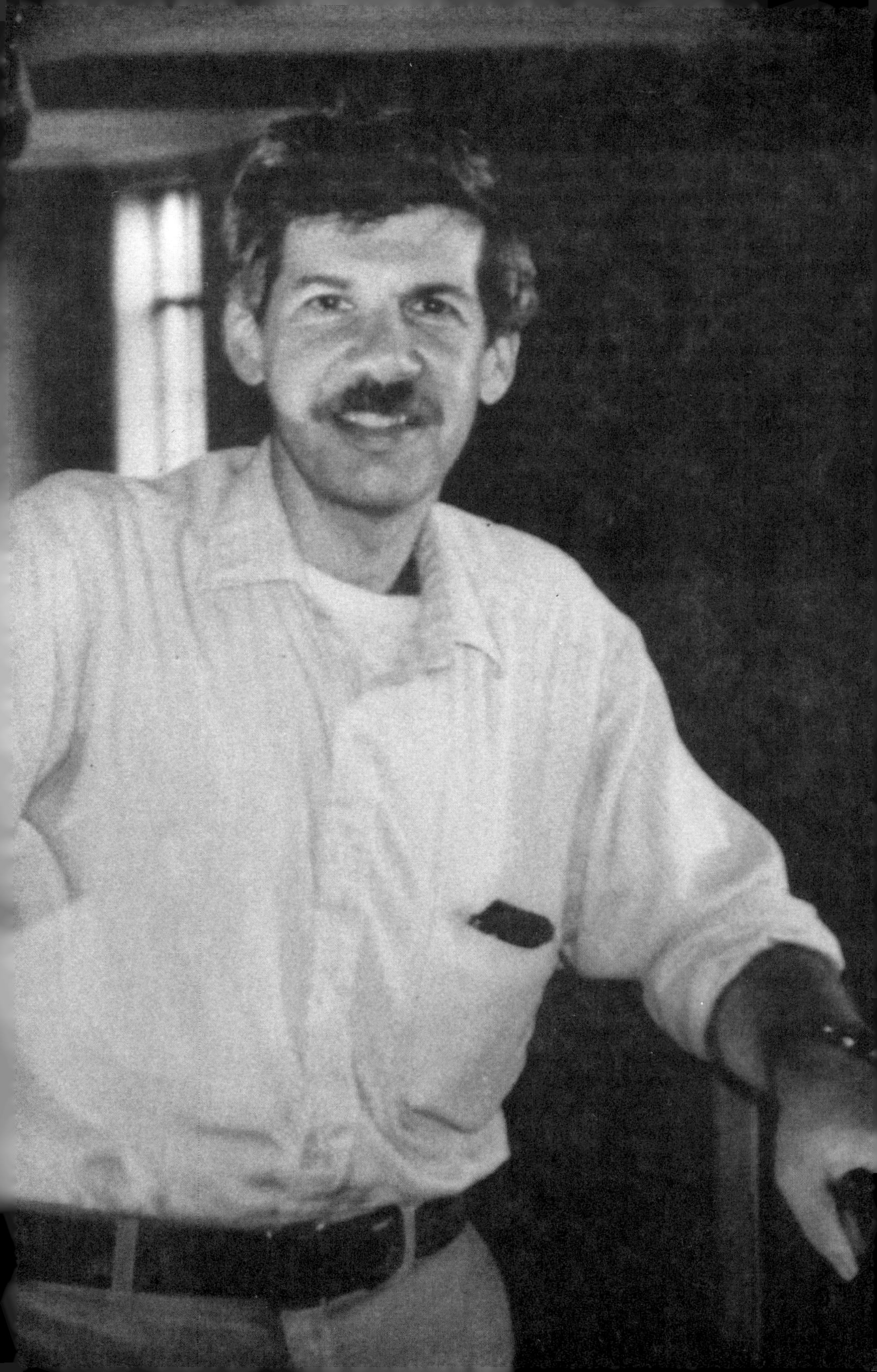

are not gradual and constant. Instead, they think that species go long periods of time—hundreds of millions of years, in some cases—without any change, and then suddenly these species undergo a comparatively short but frantic burst of evolutionary activity. In defense of this theory, they point to such species as the horseshoe crab that have remained virtually unchanged for 200 million years. Indeed, the critics claim that, if evolution worked the way the Darwinists state, then there should be more diversity among living things than actually exists.

Gould and others, however, have better evidence than a mere criticism of natural selection as the prime motive power of evolution. They point directly at the fossil record.

PRESERVED IN STONE

A **fossil** may be the bones of an animal or the body of a plant whose organic material has long since been replaced by stone. Or it may be a preserved footprint, a frozen specimen, and so on. It is any direct evidence of the existence of an organism older than ten thousand years. **Paleontologists**—scientists who study fossils—have found evidence of early bacterial life dating back 3.5 billion years (the earth itself is only 4.5 billion years old). The fossil record has gaps but has shown the expected evolutionary process: the development of more and more species.

And what does the fossil record show to support Gould and Eldredge's theory? The fossilized remains often show millions of years going by without any noticeable evolutionary change in most species. Gould and others argue that, if evolutionary change is gradual, then there should be fossilized remains showing these ongoing changes.

As an example, some 570 million years ago, life on this planet suddenly changed. For hundreds of millions of years, soft-bodied organisms had dominated the sea. Then, in a period of a few tens of millions of years—a blink of an eye in geological time—these soft-bodied creatures disappeared and were replaced by shelled organisms, as well as those with skeletons. Most of the life forms we know today arose in this frenetic burst of evolutionary activity. There was no apparent gradual change—that would have taken hundreds of millions, perhaps billions of years.

What do the natural selection advocates say to this fossil evidence or lack of it? Darwinists, such as G. Ledyard Stebbins and Francisco J. Ayala, both of the University of California at Davis, say that evolutionary changes do not necessarily show up first in structural changes, which are the ones preserved in fossilized bones. Rather, such changes may be alterations in body covering and markings. Fossilized impressions of body covering are much rarer than preserved bones, and body markings do not survive at all. The supporters of natural selection point out that archaeopteryx, the fossil link between birds and reptiles, had a skeleton that was completely reptillian, while its body cover was feathers that were birdlike.

The Darwinists also point out that their theory calls for each generation to possess only small differences from the previous one. A great many generations would go by before any major difference would be noticeable. Thus, Stebbins and others feel that the apparent stasis of many species followed by an abrupt appearance of change is an illusion. For then, the fossil record does not reveal these multitude of small changes untill a sufficient number have accumulated.

THE PATHS OF CHANGE

Despite this new theory of evolution based upon the idea of rapid, sudden change, followed by long periods of stasis, we need to note that these researchers are not saying natural selection is wrong. Rather, they see natural selection as only one of the mechanisms by which evolution occurs; to them, it is no longer evolution itself.

As Gould and others point out, however, natural selection does not really answer the question of why plants and animals adapt the way they do. For example, the Viceroy butterfly has developed a wing pattern that is similar to that of the Monarch butterfly. There is no question that this mimicry increases the Viceroy's ability to survive. To birds, Monarchs have a bad taste, and they will not usually eat them. Thus, the Viceroy survives through its protective mimicry.

But why mimicry? Rather, why not develop a taste that would discourage birds the way the Monarchs do? The process of natural selection cannot provide an answer to this question. Indeed, from the view of a Darwinist, Viceroys that tasted vile to birds might well possess a better survival trait than the mimics.

The answer lies in the butterflies' genes. Biologists have discovered that genetically it is simpler and easier for the Viceroy to have developed a new wing pattern rather than a repellent taste. Only a few gene changes were necessary in order for the Viceroy to have its pseudo-Monarch wing pattern, while large and complicated genetic changes would have been necessary to change the body chemistry of the Viceroy so that it tasted as bad to birds as did the Monarch.

Natural selection also gives one the mistaken idea that all species changes must increase survival. This is neither right nor even reasonable. Genes come in groups, and a favorable change in one gene, leading to better survival in a particular environment, will result in that gene dragging along several other genes into the general population. These others may offer nothing toward survival and, in some cases, may even be slightly detrimental.

The upright stance of humans has given us the freedom to have two of our limbs—our arms—free of the ground at all times. Our ability to use tools has been enhanced by this freedom. Yet our upright stance places stress upon both our pelvis and our spine, for which they are not fully suited, and is thus the cause of much of our back and hip problems as we grow older. Standing upright was and is a good survival trait, but it is not without its cost.

CRUCIBLES OF LIFE

Gould and others continue to search the fossil record for more evidence to support their theory of evolutionary bursts. Why was there such an evolutionary explosion 570 million years ago? John Sepkoski, a paleontologist with the University of Chicago, claims that this explosion was predictable. At this time, 570 million years ago, the earth was still primarily empty of life, and thus there were many environmental niches open. In any new environment, Sepkoski says, the growth of the population is at first slow. Then when the number of offspring reaches a sufficiently large size, the growth rate literally explodes until all of the environmental niches are filled.

Because so many possible ways existed to survive and live at this time, vast numbers of adapted individuals could find a place in the world. As the mutations and gene recombinations occurred, the organisms drifted into an appropriate niche in the environment.

Although nowhere in the fossil record is there evidence of an explosion of life forms to match that of 570 million years ago, Sepkoski and others have seen fossil evidence of the same pattern repeated at other times in the earth's past. In 1983, Sepkoski reported on his investigations of areas of the ocean in which new species arose. The popular idea had been that such new life appeared first in the comparatively hospitable, food-rich ocean deeps. Sepkoski found, however, that this was not generally true.

New marine life appears first in the more inhospitable and barren areas near the shore. Why? Sepkoski theorizes that these areas, being harsher and less populated, have available a great many more environmental niches into which new forms may fit until they have produced large enough numbers to migrate into the deeper ocean.

Showing that natural selection still has a role in this newest theory of evolution, Sepkoski feels that, because of the harshness of these shore areas, new species have to be tougher. Further, since there is less food, the marine communities in these areas are smaller, and any adaptive changes that aid survival would spread more swiftly than in other, larger populations.

Work on fossils discovered in the arctic also supports this view of harsh environments as spawning grounds for new species. Leo Hickey of Yale University reported in 1983 that he and his research team had discovered evidence of the existence of many animals and plants in the arctic long before they appeared elsewhere. Traditional wisdom has always viewed the arctic populations as having migrated from the south rather than the other way around.

According to Hickey, redwoods and birch first grew in the arctic eighteen million years before they appeared in other parts of the world, and apparently, methods of plant reproduction such as pollen production first appeared in the arctic. Large grazing animals as well as land tortoises developed in the arctic 2 million years before they began showing up in the southern latitudes.

These findings also seem to fit with human evolution. The drought that swept west central Africa some 1.5 million years ago, killing forests and leaving behind semiarid plains—less rich in food and protection—seems to mark the beginning of the evolution of our primate ancestors that led to intelligence.

No matter how much questioning of the mechanics of evolution goes on within the biological community, the reality of evolution is firmly accepted by all concerned. Gould and the Darwinists can argue over the importance of natural selection, but they do not argue over the existence of evolutionary activity. The changes proposed in evolutionary mechanics are meant only to increase our understanding. However, the nature of that understanding will probably continue to alter, particularly in the light of new fossil evidence, as well as the reevaluation of older discoveries.

CHAPTER 6
SCRUTINIZING THE FOSSIL RECORD

*H*eavy, ominous reddish-brown clouds hang oppressively over the land. Through a constant rain that burns their skin, the animals move slowly. Unable to breathe properly, one and then another drops, dying on a ground whose soil—no longer protected by the defoliated trees—has turned to powder. Even the rocks are pockmarked and dissolving.

This might be the grim future of some science fiction movie such as *The Terminator* or a model for a postnuclear-war world. But it isn't. Rather, proposed by Ronald G. Prinn of MIT, it is one possible scenario of the world of 65 million years ago, in which a comet hit the earth, bringing clouds of acid rain that eventually led to the extinction of many plant and animal species, including the dinosaurs. It is one of the recent theories claiming that periodic natural catastrophes resulted in large-scale extinctions of much of the life on this planet. Such **mass extinctions** have caught the interest of both the professional and the popular press.

Normally, we do not associate the past with the word "revolution" since revolution implies something new. But paleontologists and other scientists are discovering new information and forming new theories—whether in the lab or in the field—that are helping to create a more complete picture of how life formed and how life developed and changed on the earth.

THE RECORD SHOWS . . .

The fossil record gives us a view of the development of life on this planet (see Figure 10), but it is far from complete. Nor

Years from Present	
400,000	Modern Humans
1.5 Million	Early Humans
12 Million	Modern Mammals
26 Million	Grasses
65 Million	End of Dinosaurs
225 Million	Early Dinosaurs and Mammals
280 Million	Reptiles
300 Million	Amphibians
400 Million	Land Plants
570 Million	Shelled Marine Life
700 Million	Multicelled Plants and Soft-Bodied Marine Animals
4-3.5 Billion	Origin of Life

Figure 10. A timescale, dated from the present, showing the approximate dates of some of the major steps in evolution on this planet.

is this surprising since fossil remains needed to fill in this record are the products of accidental discoveries. Another problem arises from the difficulty in finding and recovering these artifacts. The earth's own geological activity has resulted not only in the preservation of these fossils but also in the destruction or hiding away of others. Furthermore, the best fossil-bearing sites are often in remote areas.

Difficulties aside, paleontologists have worked out the broad outlines of life's development on this planet (see Figure 10). The earliest forms of life so far discovered are bacteria that lived some 3.5 billion years ago. And for most of the existence of life on this planet, it came in the form of single-celled organisms; not until some 700 million years ago—comparatively recently in a 3.5 billion year span—did multicelled animals and plants appear. As we saw in the last chapter, the first modern multicellular life forms—particularly those having outer shells and inner skeletons—began showing up some 570 million years ago. Some 150 million years later, the first plants began moving from the sea onto the land, and not until 300 million years ago did animals make this same migration. Modern humans have only been on the planet less than half a million years.

FROM THE BEGINNING

But how and when did life begin on earth? This is a question that biologists would like to answer, but the task is a difficult one. The earth is at least 4.5 billion years old, but whether or not the recently discovered 3.5-billion-year-old bacteria are the first life on this planet will be hard to prove. Most fossils are preserved bones and other hard body parts, and soft-bodied organisms, which would be all early life since skeletons did not develop until half a billion years ago, left few fossil records.

Additionally, all the geological evidence indicates that for the first billion years of the earth's existence, the earth was bombarded by heavy showers of meteorites and asteroids. This bombardment was so massive that the earth's very crust melted, destroying any possible traces of living matter. Until 3.8 billion years ago, there is almost no geological evidence surviving, which leaves a 700-million-year gap in the earth's early history—a gap in which life's origin may well fall.

Researchers, however, have not let this lack of concrete evidence keep them from theorizing about the origins of life on the earth. Oddly enough, the very catastrophic nature of the space bombardment may have contributed to the formation of life some 4 billion years ago—only a half billion years after the earth's formation. Researchers such as David Deamer of the University of California at Davis feel that rapid cycles of hot and cold, wet and dry would have provided the necessary motive power to change nonliving chemicals into the necessary components for living things.

Deamer's theory sees life as having arisen many times in the first billion years of the earth's history. At first, as Deamer postulates, life appeared in isolated tidal pools. Each pool contained all the ingredients of life—nucleic acids, proteins, and so on. Was each pool a discrete organism? Perhaps at first, but as the pool either dried up or was flooded away, the organism died without ever having had any chance of spreading beyond the confines of its borders. It was not until the development of the cell—acting as a container for the chemicals of life—that living things began spreading over the planet.

In his lab, Deamer is trying to reproduce those early beginnings. The cell may have come from these periodic wettings and dryings. Deamer has found that lipids, which compose a significant percentage of a cell's outer membrane, once dried will in the presence of DNA engulf it when water is added. This extremely primitive structure perhaps shows us how cells began. It is, however, a long way from even the simplest modern cell, particularly when we discover that a single bacterium has two to three thousand different enzymes with half a million molecules reacting per minute.

But were the chemicals needed for the production of DNA and proteins present in the earth's early history? The answer appears to be yes. In the 1950s, Stanley Miller of the University of Chicago discharged electric sparks into a mixture of methane, ammonia, and water vapor—thought by many to have been the composition of the primal earth's atmosphere. The result was amino acids, the building blocks of proteins. Now, David Usher of Cornell University feels that these early conditions would have favored a chemical evolution—smaller molecules becoming larger until a self-replicating one arose.

Not all researchers feel that the chemical precursors of life arose on this planet; some feel they came from space. And there is some evidence to back up this view. In 1983, Cyril Ponnamperuma of the University of Maryland discovered that the five nucleotide bases necessary for DNA and RNA production were contained in the Murchison meteorite

This piece of the Murchison meteorite is 7 inches (18 centimeters) long. The Murchison meteorite contains the five nucleotides needed for RNA and DNA production in cells, evidence to some scientists that the precursors of life could have come from space.

that hit Australia in 1969. Astronomers have also discovered that large clouds of carbon-containing chemicals exist in the spiral arms of our galaxy. Some of these contain formaldehyde, which can lead to amino acids and eventually to proteins, while others have hydrogen cyanide, which can produce nucleic acids.

However, some chemists and biologists are wondering if the individual production of proteins or nucleic acids or even their presence was sufficient to produce life. Whatever its properties, DNA is not life. Without the support structures of the cell, it is just an interesting chemical. Thus, a new theory is beginning to arise, claiming that it is not the existence of either nucleic acids or proteins alone, but the actual coming together of the various chemicals of life to form the cell that was the origin of living things.

LET'S LOOK AT
THE EVIDENCE AGAIN

The search for how life on earth began may be confined to the lab, but such is not the case with the quest for other past life-forms. Paleontologists continue to have a good deal of success in this latter quest. In 1984, at Wind River Valley, Wyoming, Richard Stucky and Leonard Krishtalka of the Carnegie Museum of Natural History discovered eight new mammalian species dating from 50 million years ago. A year later, Robert Long of the University of California at Berkeley found what may be the oldest dinosaur relic—some 225 million years old—in the Petrified Forest of northern Arizona. Rarely does a year go by when paleontologists do not make such discoveries.

As important as such finds are in filling out the history of life, one of the greatest advances of paleontology in the last decade has been the reexamination and reevaluation of already documented fossils. In this process, scientists are discovering that earlier researchers often misunderstood the significance of what they had found.

In 1909, paleontologist and then secretary of the Smithsonian Institution Charles Doolittle Walcott found the Burgess Shale in western Canada. From this shale, Walcott and others removed many valuable fossils dating from 570 million years ago. However, convinced that all previous living organisms fitted well into modern groups, Walcott classified most of these animals as worms similar to earthworms.

In 1981, two British scientists, Derek Briggs of the University of Bristol and Harry Whittington of the University of Cambridge reexamined these Burgess Shale fossils. To their surprise, they discovered not only were most of Walcott's "worms" not worms at all, but they belonged to entirely new species. Indeed, three of the fossils found by Walcott and a Canadian scientist had been labeled as parts of three different organisms. Briggs and Whittington showed them actually to be part of one very large—for the time—predator.

These predators seemed to have been very important in the evolution of the life during this period. Because of their size, they posed a special threat to other, much smaller organisms. Briggs and Whittington as well as others feel that, under this predatory threat, many of the species of the period had to find new ways of surviving, such as developing shells. Some, in fact, became predators themselves. Thus, paleontologists' entire view of this world of 570 million years ago and the evolutionary pressures contained within it were changed almost overnight by this simple reexamination of fossils discovered over three-quarters of a century ago.

WARM BLOOD

Undoubtedly, the most dramatic of these paleontological reevaluations was done by Robert T. Bakker, then of Harvard University. In 1975, Bakker proposed that the classic portrait of dinosaurs as slow-moving, cold-blooded reptiles was false. Instead, according to Bakker, although dinosaurs were indeed reptiles, these animals were as warm-blooded as any present-day mammal or bird.

What do we mean when we say an animal is cold- or warm-blooded? Cold-blooded animals, such as lizards or frogs, do not produce enough internal body heat to function properly. They must raise their internal temperature by exposure to the sun—on a hot enough day, their body temperatures can be higher than those of birds or mammals. Warm-blooded animals, such as humans, dogs, or sparrows, however, have the ability to maintain a constant and efficient internal body temperature, part of which is accomplished by the insulating properties of hair or feathers.

Warm-blooded animals have certain distinctive features, one of which is bone structure. Such animals have more blood vessels running through their bones than cold-blooded ones. Upon looking closely at dinosaur bones, Bakker found that, unlike cold-blooded reptiles, they had a great many blood vessel routes: they looked very much like mammalian bones.

Another distinctive characteristic of warm-blooded animals is the ratio of predators to prey. Warm-blooded predators need to eat more to survive than cold-blooded ones. Thus, the ratio of prey to predators among warm-blooded animals is higher than that among cold-blooded ones. The size of the predator, however, makes no difference to this ratio. Cold-blooded animals such as spiders, boomer lizards, and komodo dragons all have the same predator-prey ratio, as do weasels, mice, and lions. The fossil evidence shows that the dinosaur predator-prey ratio was the same as for the warm-blooded group and not the cold-blooded one.

To test his fossil evidence, Bakker looked at the predator-prey ratio of the dimetrodon, a finback reptile, but not a dinosaur, that had cold-blooded bone structure and that flourished during the early dinosaur period. The ratio was that expected for cold-blooded predators.

Although not all paleontologists agree with Bakker, his evidence cannot be lightly dismissed. Further, as Bakker points out, warm-blooded animals can and do compete better than cold-blooded ones. If that is so, and dinosaurs were cold-blooded, how was it that mammals, appearing at least 140 million years before the dinosaurs died off, did not outcompete the dinosaurs? Until the extinction of the dinosaurs, it was they and not mammals who dominated the earth. During this period, mammals remained small and insignificant.

If, as Bakker claims, dinosaurs were warm-blooded, their dominance becomes easier to explain. Having already filled most of the earth by the time of the appearance of mammals, the dinosaurs were already well adapted to their environment. With few opportunities to expand and develop, natural selection would have limited mammals to the role of small scavengers. Only with the disappearance of the dinosaurs did mammals have their chance to become, along with birds, a major diversified group.

DISAPPEARING IN MASS

Bakker's warm-blooded dinosaur theory may provide us with a better understanding of how dinosaurs survived. Unfortunately, it does not help to explain why, after 150 million years, they suddenly died out some 65 million years ago.

But it is not just the dinosaurs. Such mass extinctions were far from rare. Some 248 million years ago—during the

Years from Present	Mass Extinction
11 Million	Mollusks
35 Million	Protozoa
65 Million	Dinosaurs
91 Million	Sea Urchins
144 Million	Ammonites
194 Million	Clams
215 Million	Various Marine Species
248 Million	Various Marine Species
570 Million	Early Soft-Bodied Marine Life

Figure 11. A timescale, dated from the present, showing some of the verified mass extinctions in the earth's past.

largest mass extinction found in the fossil record—over 90 percent of the marine species died. Figure 11 shows a number of the confirmed examples of mass extinction since then, one of the most recent being the death of large numbers of mollusks eleven million years ago. According to paleontologists John Sepkoski and David Raup of the University of Chicago, over the last 250 million years, no less than a quarter of a million marine species have died out.

What was the cause of such extinctions? Theories for the death of the dinosaurs have ranged from mammals having eaten too many dinosaur eggs to the appearance of toxic vegetation to sudden geological upheavals—mountain formations, vast shifts in land masses, volcanism. Only the latter explanation might also help account for other mass extinctions since one of the results of large-scale geological activity would be large clouds of dust that would drastically lower the earth's surface temperature.

Stegosaurus, *the armored dinosaur, is now thought to have had only one row of plates on its back, not two. This model by Stephen Czerkas is the first to represent the new "look" for this venerable beast.*

Both land and marine species would die under such circumstances. Studies by Eric Kauffman of the University of Colorado and Gerta Keller of Princeton University seem to reveal that temperature fluctuations did indeed cause the mass extinctions. Rapid temperature drops of 3.5 to 9 degrees Fahrenheit (2 to 5 degrees Celsius) would have been fatal not only to land animals but also to sealife.

COLLISION COURSE

But recently, physicist Luis Alvarez and his son, geologist Walter Alvarez, both of the University of California at Berkeley, have propsed another cause of the mass extinction of the dinosaurs. They feel that 65 million years ago, an asteroid, one of the rocky or metallic objects found in space, hit the earth. The Arizona Barringer Meteorite Crater is evidence that such events did occur in the earth's past. Even a small asteroid would hit with more force than a hydrogen bomb, and one that was 6 miles (about 10 kilometers) across would produce an explosion one hundred thousand to one million times greater than the largest nuclear bomb. Such a collision would have produced even lower surface temperatures than massive volcanic activity and would have led to large-scale death among plants and animals.

The Alvarezes' evidence? In the late 1970s, Walter Alvarez discovered that surface rocks of 65 million years ago had a very high concentration of the element iridium. This element is not normally found on the surface of the planet, but many asteroids are rich in it.

In partial confirmation of the Alvarezes' theory are the recent findings of a group of University of Chicago researchers led by Dr. Edward Anders. Examining 65-million-year-old sediment from Denmark, New Zealand, and Spain, Anders's team found traces of soot. The scientists believe that this

The Barringer meteorite crater in Arizona

soot came from large and widespread wildfires. The impact of a large asteroid would have been capable of starting such fires even hundreds of miles from its impact site. If the object struck in the Bering Sea, it could have started massive fires on three continents: Europe, Asia, and North America. The smoke from such fires would have been as deadly as the smoke from a house fire, but in this case, it would have blanketed large parts of the entire world.

NOT WITHOUT DIFFICULTY

The Alvarezes' theory, however, is not without its critics. Indeed, many paleontologists feel it does not fit the known facts about mass extinctions. For example, paleontologist William Clemens, also from the University of California at Berkeley, studied dinosaur bones and iridium deposits in eastern Montana and found that the time between the iridium being laid down and the death of the latest dinosaurs was too great a span for the events to have been related.

Indeed, according to Charles B. Officer and Charles L. Drake of Dartmouth College, the dying of the dinosaurs took between ten thousand and one hundred thousand years. No matter how great was the postulated devastation from Alvarez's hypothetical asteroid, its effects could not have lasted a fraction of ten thousand years, let alone one hundred thousand.

Officer and Drake feel that the older idea of volcanic activity is the real culprit. A period of extensive volcanism would have had much the same effect as the asteroid theory except it could have lasted ten thousand to one hundred thousand years at least. Volcanoes would also have been capable of spreading iridium by bringing it up from the earth's interior.

MAKING ROOM

Whatever the cause of these mass extinctions, their effect is much the same: the death of old species and the corresponding rise of new ones. After each extinction, opportunities exist for different organisms to expand and take over the role of the now deceased species.

After the extinction of 65 million years ago, many environmental niches were open. Where once the Tyrannosaurus preyed on other dinosaurs, now the lion stalks the zebra, the wolf the deer. Where the Pterosaur glided through the sky, now hawks, sparrows, and sea gulls fly. And where the Plesiosaur dominated the seas, the whale and the dolphin swim.

Mass extinctions obviously play a role in evolution and the creation of new species. Without such events, it seems likely that many of the marine and land species alive today would never have developed. But, of even more importance to the evolutionary scheme, mass extinctions led to a greater diversity of living things.

Although the dinosaurs died out, reptiles as a whole did not disappear; modern reptilian species are both widespread and large in number. So with the continuation of reptiles and the diversification of birds and mammals, the mass extinction of 65 million years ago created a world full of more varied organisms than had previously existed. This seems to be the general case after each mass extinction.

Scientists are still far from the final answers about how life arose and developed and changed in the earth's past. We can, therefore, expect more work, more evidence about what happened in those ancient times. Somewhere in the lab or in the ground are the answers biologists seek.

CHAPTER 7
ESTABLISHING THE NEW ORDER

None of us would argue against the basic kinship of robins, bluejays, and sparrows. We recognize all three of these species to be birds. Nor would most of us disagree that, despite their inability to fly, ostriches and penguins are also birds. But few of us would consider crocodiles and birds to be related or that birds may be among the last surviving dinosaurs. Crocodiles and dinosaurs are, after all, reptiles. However, some contemporary biologists would go so far as to lump birds, crocodiles, and dinosaurs in a group of related species, arguing that all had similar hearts and ankle joints and that wings are merely modified legs and feathers altered scales.

This is merely one manifestation of the problem that has faced biologists for centuries. How do you establish a system of classification that shows the relationships among various species? In the past, biological researchers depended upon physical similarities, such as teeth in mammals, beaks in birds, and flowers and seeds in plants, to establish related groups of organisms. But in the present, classification is based only in part on physical similarities; biologists also look for evolutionary and molecular similarities. Thus, in the last few years, classification has undergone its own revolutions to match those in other biological areas.

THE FIVE KINGDOMS

For several centuries, species were shuffled into one of three large groups or **kingdoms:** Protista (microorganisms), Plantae (plants and fungi), and Animalia (animals). Kingdoms are the largest and most general classification groups, but even for such broad categories, these three kingdoms proved to be too general. You do not have to be a biologist to see that fungi—mushrooms, mold, and so on—do not closely resemble plants. Fungi do not have the distinctive green color of plants because they lack chlorophyll, the substance that allows plants to use sunlight to convert carbon dioxide and water into glucose and oxygen.

Further, not all species of microorganisms fit well together. Indeed, they split into two different groups, One, among whose members are bacteria and blue-green algae, is very primitive, having no nucleus, no mitochondria, no protein-containing chromosomes. The other, among which are found amoebae and paramecia, is more complex, having nuclei, mitochondria, protein-containing chromosomes, and other cellular structures.

To accommodate the differences between green plants and fungi and the two groups of microorganisms, present-day biologists have created two new kingdoms: Fungi and Monera. All of the mushrooms, molds, and so on, were quickly reclassified as Fungi, while the simpler microorganisms went into Monera. Protista then contained only the more sophisticated microorganisms.

Biologists were also able to arrange this Five-Kingdom system so that it indicated basic evolutionary relationships among the five groups (see Figure 12). Monera, being the simplest living things, gave rise to the more complex single-celled species of Protista. From Protista there arose in separate but equal paths multicellular Plantae, Fungi, and Animalia. This scheme fits well the evolutionary pattern deduced from the fossil record.

Thus, the biologist used not only physical traits to arrive at the Five-Kingdom system but also molecular and evolutionary evidence. Partially because of an absence of the chemical chlorophyll, fungi were removed from Plantae and placed in their own kingdom, and because Monera were evolutionarily more primitive than Protista, they also became a separate kingdom.

```
        Plantae   Fungi   Animalia
             ↖     ↑     ↗
                Protista
                   ↑
                Monera
```

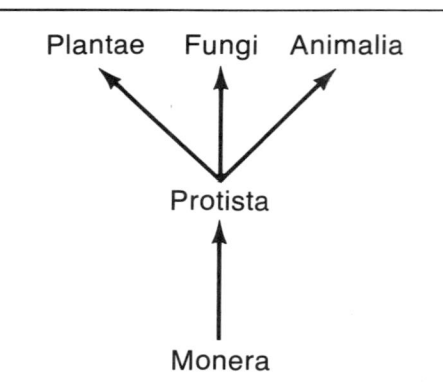

Figure 12. The Five-Kingdom Classification System of modern biology shows the evolutionary order. Monera, containing the simplest one-celled organisms, gave rise to Protista, more complex single-celled living things. From this latter arose all of the multicellular kingdoms: Plantae, plants; Fungi, mushrooms, fungus, and so on; and Animalia, animals.

FROM TOP TO BOTTOM

The kingdom is only the topmost group in the classification system, which has a hierarchy of seven major groups: kingdom, phylum, class, order, family, genus, and finally species (see Figure 13). Of this hierarchy, species is the most specific, consisting of, as we saw in Chapter 5, a population that not only shares similar physical and chemical characteristics, but that can interbreed.

 A **genus** (plural, genera), then, is made up of related species; a family consists of related genera; an order consists of related families; and so on. In Figure 13, we can see the ascending order of classification for humans. Our species is *Homo sapiens*, while our genus is *Homo*, of which all other member species, such as *Homo erectus*, are extinct. We belong to the family Hominidae and, along with great apes and monkeys, to the order Primate. Our class is Mammalia; our phylum, Chordata; and, of course, our kingdom Animalia.

ON THE CHEMICAL TRACK

In broad terms, deciding what species go into what genera, what genera go into what families, and so on, is not difficult. Common sense reveals the relationships between tigers, lions, and domestic cats, nor is it, when you begin to look, too difficult to see the similarities between the pig and the hippopotamus. But sometimes what you see may be misleading, and then molecular traits prove their value.

For over a century, biologists have been trying to decide—beyond being exotic treats for western zoo-goers—what exactly pandas are. Are they bears, which giant pandas loosely resemble? Or are they raccoons, of which lesser or red pandas are reminiscent?

Indeed, are the giant and red pandas part of the same genus? Physically, the answer appears to be yes. Each panda species has similar teeth and skull structures and similar patterns for their fur color. But if the giant panda is a bear, it possesses some important differences from the latter since pandas do not hibernate, and they bleat instead of roar.

Kingdom	Animalia
↑	
Phylum	Chordata
↑	
Class	Mammalia
↑	
Order	Primates
↑	
Family	Hominidae
↑	
Genus	*Homo*
↑	
Species	*Homo sapiens*

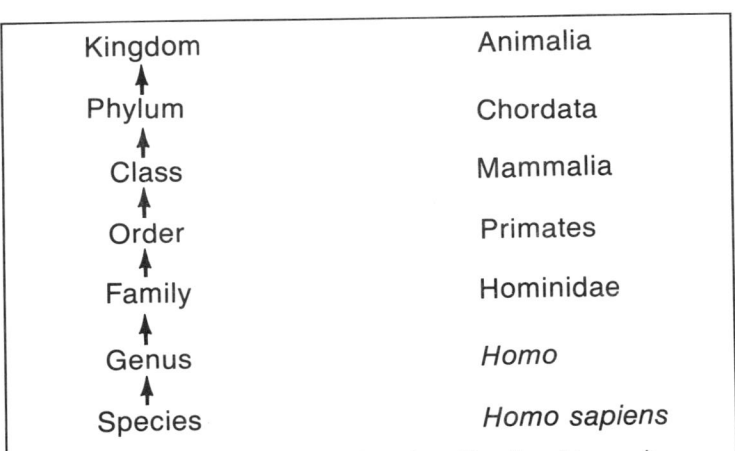

Figure 13. On the left is the classification hierarchy, running from the most general—kingdom—to the most specific—species. On the right are the hierarchial names for modern human beings.

Giant panda at the National Zoological Park in Washington, D.C. The giant panda is a bear.

The sun bear is also a bear.

Red panda at the National Zoo. The red panda is a raccoon.

This raccoon is . . .
just a raccoon.

In 1985, Stephen J. O'Brien with researchers from the Natural Zoological Park in Washington, D.C., and the National Cancer Institute set out to decide this matter once and for all by looking at the particular chemical composition of the two pandas' chromosomes, their DNA sequences, and some of their protein structures. The result? Chemically, giant pandas are definitely bears and red pandas raccoons.

So the chemical findings support the physical evidence that showed the relationship of these panda species to these other species. It, however, also demonstrated that, despite physical similarities, the two panda species were not the same genus.

But O'Brien and his colleagues were able to determine more than just panda relationships. They were also able to tell from their analysis that the giant panda split off from the bear line some 20 million years ago, while the red panda split from raccoons sometime between 30 and 50 million years ago.

And what about the seeming relationship between giant and red pandas. Have they not been closely related for over 30 million years? O'Brien feels that the physical similarities are due merely to both species retaining some of their common ancestral features. It is a physical illusion that the two are similar species.

CHEMICAL COUSINS

Such chemical analysis of DNA sequences and major protein structures have been playing an increasingly important role in showing relationships between species, as well as providing some insight as to when various species diverged from one another. Within the last decade, researchers such as biochemist Russell F. Doolittle of the University of California at San Diego have found that the more closely related two species are, the more similarities exist in the structures of their major proteins as well as their DNA sequences. Indeed, Doolittle, along with others, has been trying to work out evolutionary pathways of protein families, showing how the proteins developed and changed in order to perform their functions in various species.

For various species, such analyses are also providing a molecular clock with which to see the course of evolution. DNA analyses of humans, chimpanzees, and gorillas show that their genetic material is 99 percent the same. From this, biochemists have estimated that humans diverged from the latter two species some 5 million years ago.

How well does this figure gibe with paleontological findings? Not as well as one might hope, but not as far off as one might fear. Paleontologists see this branching as happening some 10 million years ago. The 5-million-year difference may be a result of missing or misinterpreted evidence in the fossil record, or it may be due to some yet undiscovered flaws in the molecular dating system. Still, the difference is not so great as to invalidate the molecular clock, and we can expect that, in the future, such chemical analyses will reveal more about evolutionary paths.

THE MOTHER OF US ALL?

The initial conclusion drawn from one of these chemical examinations is certainly intriguing. During the summer of 1983, Allan C. Wilson of the University of California at Berkeley reported that he had tentatively determined by chemical analysis that all living humans go back to one female ancestor, who lived some 350,000 years ago.

How did Wilson arrive at this startling conclusion? He examined mitochondrial DNA. As we saw in Chapter 2, the cell's mitochondria have their own DNA, which is different than that found in the cell's nucleus. What else is different about this DNA is that, unlike nuclear DNA in which half comes from the father and half from the mother, all mitochondrial DNA comes from the mother. This means that the only changes in this DNA are caused by mutation. The current estimate is that such mutations change the content of mitochondrial DNA a mere 2 percent every million years. By looking at the degree of mitochondrial DNA variation in over a hundred individuals scattered over the world, Wilson was about to calculate the point in time when all of this mitochondrial DNA must have been the same—that is, belonged to one female.

Such analysis can also give researchers some idea of how closely related groups of people are since the closer they are to a common female ancestor, the fewer the differences to be found in their mitochondrial DNA sequences. Interestingly, Wilson found that some Australian aborigines—a group of people who were isolated from the rest of humanity for some tens of thousands of years—are more closely related to some Asians and Africans than to other aborigines.

Perhaps work in biological classification does not seem as startling as that in genetic engineering, but this work is revealing new, often unsuspected information about living creatures, their relationships to one another, and how they evolved. This revolution—primarily a revolution in molecular biology—may have less public recognition than genetic research but is every bit as important in our overall understanding of that mystery called life.

CHAPTER 8
FINDING NEW LIFE

*E*verything is pink or pinkish-red, including the sky. The two explorers sit unmoved by this omnipresent color, merely recording it as part of the data they have come to collect. And among that data are the results of tests designed to look for life. The results? Negative. The explorers apparently have sat down in a lifeless desert.

And so, in 1976 the news came back from Mars. The Viking landers had failed to find any trace of life on the solar system's fourth planet. The failure was disappointing, but it did nothing to dampen the biological interest in discovering life beyond our planet.

People have always been fascinated by discoveries of new life, particularly animals. When Europeans began exploring the rest of the world in the fifteenth century, the strange animals the explorers discovered in the Americas, Africa, Asia, and Australia attracted as much attention and curiosity as any single part of these men's accounts. Like earlier peoples, most of us today are equally intrigued by the idea of new life, whether on this planet or another, and it is not surprising that biologists of our century have continued searching for and finding new species.

*ANYTHING NEW
UNDER THE SUN?*

With the earth being the home of several million species—current estimates place insect species alone at thirty million—it is not surprising when biologists occasionally discover a new one. In most cases, however, these are closely

—89

related to those with which we are already familiar. The late paleontologist George Gaylord Simpson pointed out that of the 126 mammalian species discovered in the twentieth century, over 75 percent of them were either bats or rodents.

Simpson went on to add that two-thirds of these species were discovered prior to 1930. Why have so few new species been discovered in the last fifty-seven years of our century as compared to the first thirty? According to Simpson, the species found in the twentieth century were very small populations in very isolated and remote areas of the world. In other words, they were difficult to find because they were difficult to reach. There are fewer and fewer such regions every year on the earth, and thus fewer places for unknown species to hide.

But does all this mean that there are no truly new and unique life-forms for contemporary biologists to find and to study? Not at all. Obviously, the search is more difficult and the discoveries rarer, but present-day biologists have found new life. These new species, however, are proving to be more than curiosities, for they are revealing unsuspected methods of survival. Each one seems to broaden the biologist's perception of the versatility of life.

INTO THE DEPTHS

A mile and a half (almost 2.5 kilometers) beneath the ocean's surface, the research submarine *Alvin* moves in a strange world lit only by *Alvin*'s own lights. At this depth, there is no natural light, for sunlight only penetrates about 600 feet (180 meters) down. After that depth, the darkness—and with it the sunless cold—of the ocean's deeps closes in, as it has for the past several billion years.

The sun. It is at the beginning of our earthly food chain. Green plants turn the energy of sunlight into food for themselves. Then animals eat the plants, thus surviving on secondhand solar energy. And, of course, other animals eat these plant-eaters; their energy comes thirdhand, but it is still from the sun. No matter how far down you follow the surface food chain, you can always follow it back to the sun.

So, although earlier in the century, not knowing what

might lie on the deep ocean floors, people postulated fanciful creatures—huge and armored against the immense pressure exerted by thousands of feet (hundreds of thousands of meters) of water—the reality was no real surprise to marine biologists, those who study underwater life. What else could one expect of a sunless environment? What the first deep-sea explorers found: lifeless, twisting canyons lined with the silt of centuries.

At least, they seemed lifeless until 1979 when, aboard the *Alvin*, oceanographer John Baross of Oregon State University and colleagues began exploring the Central Pacific Ridge which is 1.5 miles (2.5 kilometers) deep. The explorers found life—in fact, they found a whole colony of organisms clustered around a group of hot-water vents. The area was covered with clamlike animals and worms almost 5 feet (1.5 meters) long. And in the hot water surrounding the vents were bacteria.

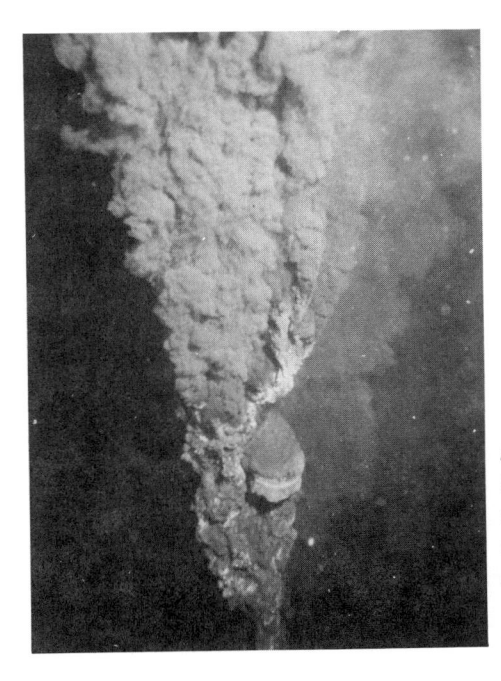

Black smoker in the East Pacific Rise. Many new organisms have been discovered living around underwater hot-water vents such as this one.

—91

Scanning electron micrograph of a worm collected from a black smoker like the one in the previous photograph (1µ=0.000001 meter)

This discovery was the first evidence that life could exist on the earth that did not depend upon energy from the sun. Since then, Baross and others have found similar hot-vent colonies in the Atlantic Ocean.

THE POWER FROM WITHIN THE EARTH

How could these creatures survive? Because of geothermal energy—heat generated by volcanic activity or hot springs. The underwater hot-water vents are similar to the geysers of Yellowstone National Park.

The water jetting out of these underwater vents is between 630 degrees Fahrenheit (350 degrees Celsius) and

—92

720 degrees Fahrenheit (400 degrees Celsius). Such temperatures are sufficient to keep the water temperature at a livable level for some distance from these heat sources.

Biologists have yet to work out the complete mechanism of these geothermal life-forms, particularly since these organisms are so difficult to reach for study. The scientists feel confident that at the bottom of this deep-sea food chain are the bacteria living in the water surrounding the hot-water vents. The bacteria survive by eating sulfur, with which this hot water is rich. The microorganisms convert this sulfur into energy, which they can use to keep themselves alive.

The clamlike creatures then eat the bacteria. Thus, the bacteria perform the same function in this geothermal community as green plants do in solar-based communities.

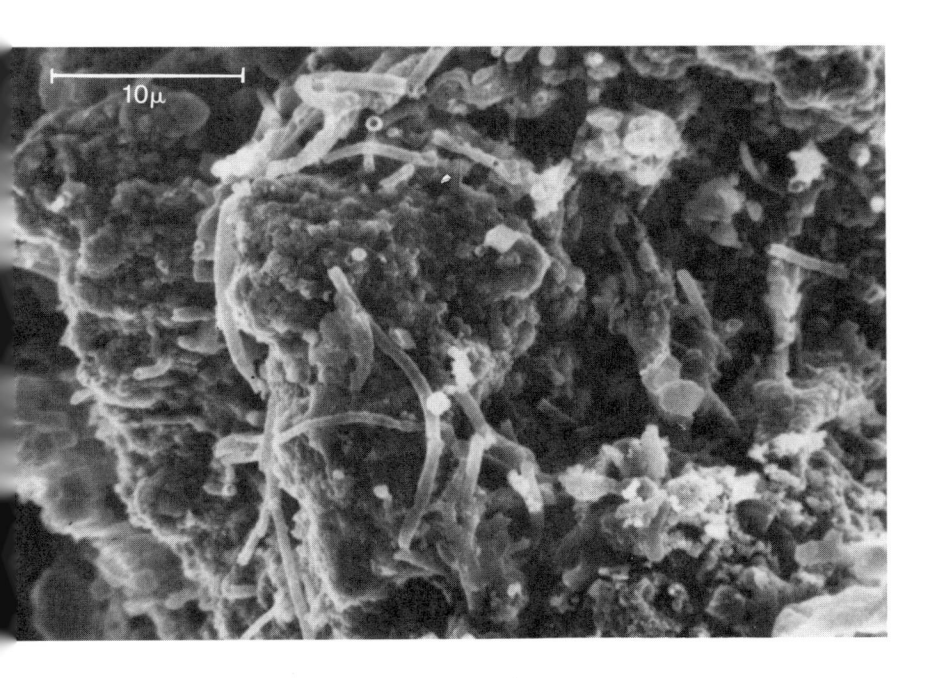

Scanning electron micrograph of microorganisms growing on rocks near a black smoker

These sulfur-eating bacteria are of interest for more than their geothermal existence. They live in water that is 450 degrees Fahrenheit (250 degrees Celsuis), which is two and one-half times the boiling point of water. Baross is presently attempting to duplicate the hot-vent conditions in his laboratory so that he can grow such bacteria for study. He would very much like to find out how these organisms can withstand temperatures that are at least twice those in which any surface bacteria can live.

Nor is the mystery of this deep-sea life at an end. Biologists are also puzzled by the long worms, for they are not sure what these worms eat or even how. None of these creatures has a mouth. Investigators, however, noticed that more than half the length of each worm is covered with a tissue and that in this tissue are swarms of bacteria. Currently, biologists think that these bacteria process chemicals from the surrounding waters and pass on part of these to the worms as food.

This deepwater community has shown biologists that a food chain may depend upon something other than solar energy. It is much too early to tell in what directions this discovery will take biologists, but already some researchers are speculating that early forms of life on this planet may have been dependent upon geothermal energy and not solar.

DEEP PLANTS

The ocean deeps are by no means through presenting biologists with surprising new species, as Mark M. Littler of the Smithsonian Institution's Museum of Natural History discovered. For most of us, algae is something we put in our fish tanks or see washed up on a beach. Yet it is one of the more important foodstuffs for many marine animals. Also, marine biologists considered it as fully dependent upon sunlight as any other plant. True, some species can get along fine with only 1 percent of the sunlight that reaches the surface, but until 1984 no one thought any plant could survive on less.

Littler, however, found differently. At over 800 feet (260 meters), Littler discovered a flourishing colony of red algae on an undersea mount near the Bahamas. At this depth, the sunlight reaching the seamount was only 0.0005 percent of that at the surface. These plants proved to be 100 percent more efficient at capturing light and using it than other previously known species. Littler also suspects they may have other energy sources, but there is no doubt that they do use light.

The cells of the algae are stacked in columns; to these cells, the plants have added an extra layer—made out of limestone—to the vertical walls. Much like water through a drainpipe, any light hitting one of these columns passes through all the cells, even reaching the farthermost bottom ones.

Littler sees no reason to assume that these plants are unique since the particular seamount he explored was not. He feels confident that future algae colonies will be discovered at equal depths.

THE SMALLEST OF THE SMALL

Not all new life-forms are discovered in the ocean. Indeed, some may lurk in our very bodies. As we have seen, viruses are small RNA- or DNA-filled microorganisms that use other cells' genetic material to reproduce. Until the early 1970s, researchers thought that the virus was the tiniest possible organism, but then they discovered viroids, which are nothing more than a naked strand of RNA.

But that was not the end. In the early 1980s, P. Prusiner of the School of Medicine at the University of California, San Francisco, found **prions**. Prions are suspected of being the cause of certain nervous system diseases, particularly the rare disease that killed famed choreographer George Balanchine. There is also some evidence that they may be involved with Alzheimer's disease, a nervous disorder leading to rapid senility and eventual death.

But prions possessed a completely unprecedented trait: unlike viruses and viroids, prions do not appear to have RNA. In fact, to date, no one has been able to discover any nucleic acid associated with them. They seem to be pure protein.

Does this mean that biologists may have to re-think their ideas about genes and cell reproduction? No, not completely, but if it does turn out that prions do completely lack nucleic acids, then some modifications will be in order. Certainly, these smallest of the small have started biologists looking for theories to describe their reproductive process.

Prusiner, however, is not quite ready to admit that prions have no RNA or DNA. He feels that, because of their extremely tiny size, whatever RNA they might have would be so minuscule as to escape chemical detection. The prion's protein coat consists only of some 250 amino acids (compared to the hundreds of thousands in the average protein) and thus might only need a nucleic acid with fifty nucleotides.

Prusiner also postulates that even if the prion lacks a nucleic acid, it could reproduce itself without resorting to some new form of reproduction. Genes are turned on by enzymes, which are nothing more than proteins. Possibly the invading prion acts as such an enzyme, attaching itself to a specific gene and activating it. The gene would then direct the production of proteins, which would themselves be prions.

BEYOND THE EARTH

The earth is only one planet among nine in our solar system and, if astronomical theory is correct, one among billions in our galaxy. It is not surprising, therefore, that some biologists would begin to wonder about the possibility of **extraterrestrial life**—any species not native to the earth. Such biologists, known as **exobiologists**, have even begun to search for traces of life beyond earth. To date, this search has yet to turn up any direct evidence of alien life, but there are suggestive clues hinting at the possible existence of such life.

As we saw in Chapter 6, researchers have discovered the five nucleotides needed for DNA and RNA synthesis inside at least one meteoroid. Additionally, astronomers have detected, floating in interstellar space, clouds of carbon-containing chemicals that could form the basis for living matter.

Also floating in space are small particles that have led the famous British astronomer Sir Fred Hoyle and his co-worker

Chandra Wickramasinghe to theorize that not only is there extraterrestrial life but also that terrestrial life began when the earth was seeded from space. The two astronomers propose that the small space particles were those seeds, some of which fell to earth some four billion years ago. They claim that various tests show that these grains have physical similarities to *E. coli* bacteria. And according to another researcher, P. J. Kushner of the University of Ottawa in Canada, microorganisms could survive the conditions of interstellar space, although they could not have evolved there.

ALIENS' HOME?

What exobiologists would like is to find an actual alien specimen. Since we lack the capacity to reach even our nearest stellar neighbor, this means searching the planets and moons in our solar system. Except for earth, the solar system does not seem a likely place for life—or at least earthlike organisms. Still, this view may be too pessimistic.

And where would we look? Should it be Mars again, since the Viking landers examined only two spots on the planet's surface and since some scientists have criticized the validity of the tests they ran?

But the best candidate may be Venus. Venus might seem an unlikely place to seek life, particularly in light of the data from various probes over the last two decades. The surface of the second planet is a raging inferno, plagued by gigantic storms and constant volcanic activity.

Life, however, does not have to live on the surface of a planet. It might instead live in Venus's upper atmosphere among the cloud layers. And here Venus is comparatively mild, indeed earthlike in temperature. These upper cloud layers also have water vapor, carbon dioxide, nitrogen, and sunlight, all the ingredients necessary for plant life. If there is life on Venus, it probably exists continually swimming in the atmosphere, as fish do in the waters of earth.

Nor is Venus the only possible home for extraterrestrial life in the solar system. The upper atmosphere of Jupiter may also provide the right conditions for life—a floating life akin to that postulated for Venus. Or perhaps single-celled plants live on the ice that covers Jupiter's moon Europa. Or perhaps we should look under the ice surfacing Titan, Saturn's largest moon, where a life-bearing ocean may roll.

THE CONTINUING QUEST

Obviously, without any evidence of life beyond earth, biologists cannot really know what alien life might be like. Such a life-form could well have evolved in an entirely different direction from terrestrial life. Indeed, two of the presently unanswerable questions in biology are whether or not life must be carbon-based and whether or not it must possess nucleic acids. Could silicon—an atom chemically related to carbon—provide the basis for life? Could there be such a thing as a chlorine-based organism? An alien species might provide answers to these questions and to others. It would certainly tell us a great deal about what is and what is not universal about life.

The search for new life is based upon more than idle curiosity. As we have seen, new species teach biologists new biological lessons; they provide new insights into the ways organisms stay alive. Of course, not all new species teach us new things, but those that do often open up unsuspected avenues of exploration. For this reason, we can expect biologists to continue the search for new life on land, in the ocean, and even in space.

CHAPTER 9
TRACING THE WEB OF LIFE

While some biologists continue to search for new life, others seek to understand how organisms and their environments interrelate. Such study is **ecology,** and it is of great importance because, over the last twenty years, we have become increasingly aware of humanity's effect upon the complex and fragile biological web that encompasses the globe. For the most part, this effect has been bad: polluted air, water, and soil; endangered species; and destroyed habitats.

Just how grave is our human threat to the earth's ecological network? What has been our actual effect upon it? What will be the future consequences of our present-day actions or inactions? Is there anything that can be done to halt or slow environmental damage? These are questions needing answers, but because of the complexity of ecological interrelationships, ecologists are only now beginning to find these answers—and only partial answers at that. Still, it is in their increasing ability to present us with even tentative answers that the current revolution in ecology lies. Further, out of this work, ecologists have created the foundation for a new biological discipline: conservation biology.

ENVIRONMENTAL IMPACT

One of the gravest problems human activity poses to the world's ecology is pollution. Since the beginning of the Industrial Revolution in the last century, human factories have dumped hundreds of thousands of tons of chemical waste into the air, the ground, the water. All of this is now having its effect on our environment.

—*99*

Within the last decade, ecologists and others have become increasingly concerned with one particular form of air pollution—acid rain due to human pollution. **Acid rain** forms when various compounds such as sulfur dioxide are emitted by industrial smokestacks. These pollutants combine with water in the air to form acid, a corrosive chemical, which later falls to the surface as rain.

According to the most recent studies, acid rain is destroying trees and perhaps animal life in eastern Canada, the northeastern United States, and Europe. In 1984, Arthur Johnson of the University of Pennsylvania noted that acid rain had killed 50 to 70 percent of high-elevation red spruces in West Germany and northeastern North America. In 1983, the National Academy of Sciences reported that, by reducing industrial emissions of sulfur dioxide, we would reduce the amount of acid rain.

Vegetation damaged by acid rain

But biologists have recently discovered that the sulfur dioxide threat to plants is more complicated than merely its direct effect as acid rain. Three British researchers, G. P. Dohmen, S. McNeill, and J. N. B. Bell, found that this chemical increases the rate of growth of some insect pests, as well as their activity. Insects such as the black bean aphid and the Mexican bean beetle seem to thrive on sulfur dioxide. When exposed to sulfur dioxide, the latter produces twice as many eggs as normal.

And to illustrate further the complexity of the effects of air pollution, John C. Liment and Bayne Thompson of Cornell University found that some plants produce chemicals that protect them from these airborne toxins. Ironically, these same chemicals make the plants tastier to insect predators.

TOO WARM

Over the past two decades, scientists have begun worrying about the buildup of another chemical in the atmosphere: carbon dioxide. Although carbon dioxide is the same gas all animals breathe out, it is also produced in large quantities by burning coal and oil. As these large amounts of carbon dioxide accumulate in the atmosphere, it may be, as some researchers fear, triggering off the **greenhouse effect.** Scientists believe that, because of its chemical properties, large amounts of carbon dioxide in the air act as an insulating blanket, keeping ground heat from escaping into space and thus raising the temperature at the earth's surface. The earth would eventually become like the inside of a greenhouse.

Using evidence from the fossil record and observations of living species, ecologists feel that such a global warming would have particularly severe effects upon certain species. The paleontological record shows that in the past, when such warming trends occurred, species migrated farther north to cooler environments. In the past, however, these temperature rises were slow, taking hundreds or thousands of years. If human pollution results in a greenhouse effect, it will be upon us and all species within the first few decades of the next century. The time for gradual adjustments will not exist.

Ecologists fear that many species will die in such a sudden warming. Any species that eats only one type of animal or plant is in grave danger. For instance, the everglade kite feeds exclusively on the apple snail. If Florida became too warm for either species to survive, the kite could easily fly north. It would, however, do this bird little good if its only food source was too slow—and even the fastest-moving snail covers very little ground even in the course of a year—to make the same journey safely. The result might be two extinct species.

Migratory species would also be hard hit. First, many of them, particularly birds, will have to travel through the hottest parts of the world since many such species go from the northern to the southern hemisphere. Second, many breeding grounds will no longer be available because they will lie in regions that are too hot for the species to survive.

MUCKING ABOUT

As with any branch of science, ecology requires new techniques in order to discover new facts. For ecologists to understand fully the effects of human activity upon the environment and to create models capable of predicting future consequences of that activity, they must first find ways to study the relationships existing between various species. It is a difficult enough task on a local level, let alone on a global one. Yet these scientists are constantly testing ways to investigate ecological systems.

During 1984, in the Great Sippewissett Marsh near Falmouth, Massachusetts, David J. Peterson of the Marine Biological Laboratory worked out a way to discover whether all ribbed mussels living in the area ate the same thing or whether their diet varied from spot to spot. Peterson, as had others before him, assumed that logically the diet would vary according to what food was immediately available, but no one had ever actually proven this assumption.

No matter how sound an assumption appears, scientists prefer to have proof. More than one such assumption has turned out to be wrong because of some previously unknown factor. And the very process of discovering the true state of things is the arrow that finally led to the identification of that factor.

Peterson's proof involved supplying radioactive sulfur, carbon, and nitrogen or nutrients for marsh grasses and plankton—one-celled microscopic plants and animals washed into the marsh by tides from nearby Buzzards Bay. The ratio of the three radioactive atoms differed between marsh grass and plankton, so Peterson had a way of specifically identifying the source of mussel food.

As Peterson and others expected, the mussels nearest Buzzard's Bay had a diet consisting mostly of plankton. Those farthest from the bay ate mostly particles of marsh grasses.

Peterson put in several months' worth of work to verify the interrelationships between just a few species in a small marshland. Imagine the effort it would take to discover the connections between all of the hundreds of species in this one marsh. Now multiply that by the entire world, and you begin to see the magnitude of the task facing ecologists.

OBSERVING FROM THE HIGH GROUND

What is needed for large-scale ecological investigations is some method of quickly gathering information about large areas of the world. And for certain studies, that method now exists in orbit around our planet: artificial satellites. Scientists such as Compton J. Tucker of NASA's Goddard Space Center have begun relying on the National Oceanic and Atmospheric Administration's weather satellites and the Landsat satellites. Although none of these satellites was designed specifically to examine ecological systems, they all have detection systems flexible enough to be used to provide data about the vegetation cover of our planet.

Prior to satellite surveys, which began only in the early 1980s, several individuals would set out and record the number of tree and plant species to be found in a certain area. After a lengthy and sometimes difficult correlation of these reports, scientists would have an idea of whether the area's vegetation was expanding, contracting, or remaining the same.

Orbital surveys have proven to be just as accurate as those made by people on the ground. Also, satellite surveys are less expensive, and they are faster—a ground survey takes weeks, sometimes months, to complete, while a satellite can gather everything in one pass over the area in question.

Tucker and others are very interested in following the fluctuations in vegetation growth, particularly those caused by human activity. Such fluctuations have important effects not only upon local environments but also on regional—and probably global areas. Because large areas of vegetation can die rapidly, the more timely the data, the more likely adverse conditions can be spotted.

A LITTLE RAIN

Such studies are also providing ecologists with their first full picture of the relationship between the amount of vegetation in an area and its rainfall. In 1980, a nineteen-month Landsat study of northern Africa showed that it is not just the more rain, the greater the number of plants and trees, and the less rain, the fewer the number of plants and trees. Additionally, Landsat data revealed that the loss of trees and plants in a region led to a corresponding drop in rain.

The Amazon rain forest is an excellent example of how this process works. Originally, of all the water that fell as rain in the Amazon, most of it was sucked up by trees and plants, which eventually released this water back into the air through transpiration. The remaining rainfall returned to the atmosphere by evaporation. All of this water was now free to fall once more as rain, and so the cycle continued.

Tropical forest in Brazil. Are any forests near you this lush? Is there a relationship in your area between the amount of vegetation and the amount of rainfall?

—104

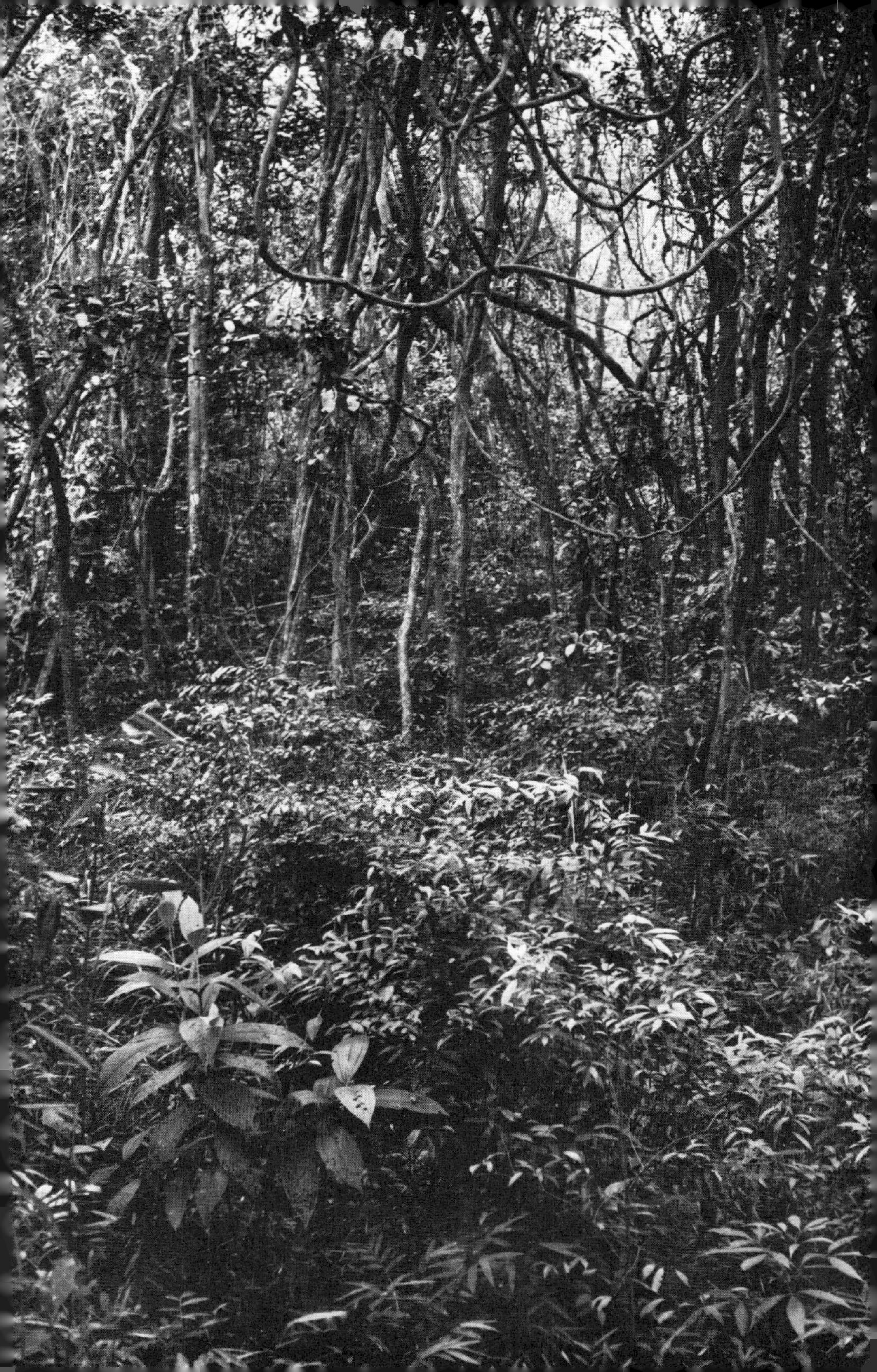

At least it was until humans began cutting down the trees and clearing the forest for farms and towns. Satellite data show that, as the number of trees and plants decrease in the Amazon, so does the amount of water returned to the atmosphere. There is not enough vegetation to maintain the cycle at its former level. As a result, more and more of the water, instead of passing through plants on the way back into the air, runs down to rivers and streams and is carried out of the region.

The result in the Amazon? As rainfall decreases, more plants and trees die of thirst, thus letting more water escape out of the region through runoff. And this new cycle is leading to higher temperatures, more soil erosion, and climatic changes all over Brazil. Indeed, the decrease in rainfall in the Amazon is drying out not only parts of Brazil but also parts of Paraguay. The ultimate end will be deserts in onetime lush areas of central South America. Similar rainfall changes in Africa, India, and China are also producing deserts.

CONSERVATION BIOLOGY

Studying ecology teaches one some grim lessons and presents a sometimes equally grim future. However, even for a young science, ecology is producing scientists who do more than observe. They are involved in their own revolution: they act whenever possible and in whatever manner is appropriate to save both species and ecological systems.

In 1981, western New Guinea faced a crisis. Because of increasing logging operations and a growing human population, much of the wildlife in this part of the island was faced with extinction. The authorities wanted to save these endangered species, but at the same time, their economy was dependent upon the very growth that was leading to this mass death.

The solution came from a conservation biologist, who suggested the immediate formation of a series of natural parks in the highlands of New Guinea, which the logging and human population had yet to invade. Such is the work of this new breed of ecologist. A biological generalist, the conservation biologist attempts to save large animal and plant populations from extinction. These ecological troubleshooters have to be well versed not only in population biology, genetics, environmental monitoring techniques, veterinary medicine, and biogeography but also in nonbiological disciplines, such as sociology, anthropology, and natural resource management. For it is the job of the conservation biologist to find a solution to an ecological crisis, and such solutions normally involve human interests and needs as well as plant and animal survival.

The conservation biologist, however, is not concerned with saving all species in an area. Rather, he or she operates on the basis that those species that provide the most diversity in the population and that offer the greatest future genetic potential are the ones that must be saved. Often, this means that the populations that come under these ecologists' management are those that are the largest in a particular environment, although not always since species variety is also absolutely essential.

Although still a relatively new discipline, conservation biology has been successful in several areas. It has been responsible for the design and management of wildlife areas such as those in western New Guinea, the supervised breeding of endangered species, and the artificial maintenance of some two thousand species of mammals and birds in zoos. Without such efforts, many more species might well have joined the list of extinct ones than already have.

Ecology is still an area of biology filled with more unknowns then knowns, but a full understanding of ecological processes is an absolute necessity if we are not to lose most of the world we see around us today. Information and timely action in this field are truly a matter of life and death, not only for all the other species that inhabit our world but possibly for us as well.

CHAPTER 10
LOOKING FROM THE INSIDE OUT

There is often a thin line dividing biology from the other sciences. Indeed, it is quite legitimate to consider a field such as biochemistry to be part of chemistry as well as of biology. But of all the disciplines with which biology is allied, perhaps the most controversial, and certainly newest, is sociology.

In 1975, Harvard biologist Edward O. Wilson with his **sociobiology** created a new biological science and a revolution. According to Wilson, human behavior, particularly as seen in human culture, has a genetic basis. Sociobiology, then, is the study of the relationship between human genes and human culture.

THE BIOLOGY OF CULTURE

Certainly there is nothing unusual or new about researchers using studies of animal behavior to shed light on human psychology. Psychologist Ronald Nadler of the Yerkes Regional Primate Research Center in Atlanta, Georgia, has been watching the abnormal actions of some female gorillas who physically abuse their young. He is hoping these observations will give him some insight into human child abuse. At the other end of the country, another psychologist, William Mason of the California Primate Research Center in Davis, California, uses monkeys to learn more about the effects of stress on people.

Researchers have even gone so far as to compare the social structures within honeybee hives and ant colonies to those of human societies, although more as a device to

Honeybees have a high degree of social organization. Some scientists see useful parallels between insect societies and human societies.

understand these insects than to offer insights into human sociology.

It is on the basis of such ideas and work that Edward Wilson—whose specialty is the study of insects—proposed sociobiology. But the sociobiologists need not look at other animals' behavior (although at times they do); they need look only at their fellow humans, particularly at their cultures. Although few anthropologists or sociologists would question that the behavior of other species is ruled by genes, most of them refuse to believe that human behavior is a genetic product. For them, modern humans behave as their various complex societies dictate.

Wilson, however, believes that human beings have too many behavioral patterns in common—ones that cut across cultural lines—for there to be anything but a genetic origin. He points out that all humans, no matter what their culture—European, Asian, African—see and recognize the same colors. The word may be different in different languages, but blue is always blue; red, red; and so on.

Further, with few exceptions, facial expressions are universal among people. Take photographs of expressions such as grief, anger, laughter, and happiness, and people from all cultures recognize them.

Wilson does not claim, however, that any one person's genes predetermine his or her behavior. All the genes do is to supply a bias for some particular form of conduct, but such a bias can be, and sometimes is, overruled by an individual who wishes to act in a different way.

Some anthropologists, such as Marvin Harris of the University of Florida, concede that early human behavior might well have been genetic in origin, but no longer. Harris thinks that, for at least the past ten thousand years, human culture has been the primary source of human conduct. He points out that this period marks explosive changes in human social orders, beginning with the invention of agriculture, running through the creation of political states, and coming up to the present industrial revolutions. To Harris, the stretch of time for this series of major and radical human developments seems much too short to have arisen from a genetic-cultural evolution.

THE CULTURAL ENVIRONMENT

Undaunted by such critics, Wilson and other sociobiologists, such as David Barash of the University of Washington, continue to work out their theories. At the root of sociobiology is the premise that genes create in humans similar mental, physical, and chemical responses to the general environment. According to Wilson and Barash, these responses eventually give rise to cultural traditions, and these cultural traditions then become part of the environment. Through natural selection, this cultural environment favors individuals whose minds will most likely accept and operate within the specific culture.

In effect, sociobiologists see a particular human culture and genes as having set up a closed cycle that feeds back upon itself. The genes support the culture, and the culture encourages the inheritance of those same genes.

As an example, let us look at cooperation. It would be difficult to discover a human society that did not place a high value on cooperation among its own members. But does cooperation have a genetic basis? Sociobiologists would argue yes since it is found in many other species besides humans: great apes show cooperative behavior, and so do wolves and lions as well as bees and ants.

For those species that show cooperative behavior, it provides survival advantages to the individuals of each group. A cooperative group finds it easier to detect, avoid, and defend against predators than a lone individual. The group can put out scouts, relieving the rest of the group to hunt for food or to sleep, and they can organize mass attacks against enemies. Further, such groups normally will have less difficulty in finding food than an individual since they can cover a larger area more quickly.

Assuming, therefore, that cooperative behavior is genetic, then the sociobiologist would say that very early human cultures established rules to reward such behavior. Cooperative members would have received a fair share of the food and enjoyed the group's protection from natural enemies.

Those who were not cooperative would have been

punished either by being pushed to the outskirts of the group or expelled. In either case, such individuals would have been less likely to eat well and would have been more likely to fall prey to predators.

Since the cooperatively-minded individuals would have had the greatest chance at survival, they would also have been the ones most likely to breed. Eventually then, through natural selection, those who followed the cultural rules of cooperation would have passed this disposition down to their descendants, making it a genetic as well as a cultural behavior.

THROUGH OTHERS' EYES

If sociobiologists had a way of actually studying early humans, they might be able to determine the validity of sociobiology. Since they cannot study our remote ancestors, they must look for other animal species to provide those insights. Biologists such as Michael P. Ghiglieri feel that the study of monkeys and great apes, particularly chimpanzees, can show us some of the evolutionary forces that shaped human nature.

Begining in 1977, Ghiglieri spent two years studying wild chimpanzees in western Uganda. Chimpanzees are the closest biological relatives to humans—the DNA of the two species varies only by 1 percent. Therefore, it is not surprising that chimpanzees have a social order similar to that of early humans.

Like those humans, a group of chimpanzees stakes out a forage territory. At the beginning of each day, the group splits up, and the individual members hunt for food, reassembling later in the day. Other ape species forage in specific territories, but at all times, they, depending upon their species, hunt either as a full group or as individuals. Only chimpanzees and humans live in groups, but forage as individuals.

Chimpanzees have another trait that sets them apart from other apes and places them with humans. When a female chimpanzee finally matures, she does not mate with any of her own group. Instead, like women in early human societies, she leaves her group and finds another.

Just how far the similarity between chimpanzee and human social orders goes, no one, including Ghiglieri, knows. However, there are enough parallels between early humans and their nearest great ape relatives that Ghiglieri feels that chimpanzee studies may eventually give us clues as to how human behavior formed.

Chimpanzees at the North Carolina Zoological Park in Asheboro

SOCIAL ENGINEERING

While Ghiglieri studies wild chimpanzees, Edward Wilson has begun proposing a more active role for sociobiology, one that goes beyond merely studying the possible relationship between human culture and human genetics. Feeling that sociobiology presents humanity with an opportunity to use cultural pressure to eliminate certain kinds of human behavior, he thinks it is time to consider social engineering.

Wilson claims that modern humans carry many behavioral patterns left over from prehistoric times and that these behaviors pose a real threat to us in the nuclear age. He points to aggression and fear of strangers as to such examples. Wilson sees no other real alternative to dealing with these particular human cultural problems except through social engineering.

In order to accomplish, as Wilson proposes, an end to aggression, sociobiologists would have to create cultural traditions that would select individuals who were not aggressive. These people then would provide the genes for later generations and the beginning of the closed cycle of that nonaggressive culture.

Not surprisingly, this social engineering proposal of Wilson's has met with opposition, even within the ranks of sociobiologists. First, most of Wilson's colleagues feel that too little is known about the sociobiology of humans to make such engineering possible. Second, they fear that opportunistic governments would use such social engineering to create docile citizens.

THE NATURAL ORDER

Certainly, if the nature of revolution is to challenge and overthrow conventional wisdom, Wilson with his theory of sociobiology and his proposal for social engineering has done so. Whether or not he or his sociologist critics are correct, only time will tell. It is unlikely that either position will remain unchanged through the heat of the debate, and the probable outcome may well be a new synthesis of biological insight and sociological observation. Out of that may arise the beginnings of a true understanding of human behavior and culture.

Out of such understanding, we can only hope all humanity benefits.

As we have seen, Wilson's revolution is only one of many in the biological sciences. Indeed, biology is a science currently undergoing constant, sometimes radical, changes. Nothing could be more appropriate for the discipline whose focus is life, for what else in our known universe displays more varied change than life? Change: that is the natural order of the living.

Some of these changes will directly affect us as DNA manipulation continues and becomes increasingly sophisticated and as ecologists learn more about the balance of life on our planet. Others, such as the search for new life, will probably not be of immediate importance to us but will on occasion pique our interest. Still, no matter what we end up doing with our lives, every time we look at a bird, watch a butterfly, observe a squirrel, we will at that moment be biologists.

GLOSSARY

Acid Rain. Rain made acidic by the interaction of various natural or manmade substances and water in the atmosphere.

Amino Acids. Any of a group of nitrogen-containing chemicals that are the units composing proteins.

Biology. The study of all aspects of living creatures: their behavior, structure, chemical nature, environment, heredity, evolution.

Biotechnology. The use of living creatures as well as natural or synthesized DNA, RNA, or proteins to manufacture new drugs, to create new medical procedures, to improve agricultural production, and so on.

Cancers. Wild, uncontrolled growths of cells.

Cell. The basic structural and functional unit of all living things. Each cell contains nuclear material, in which resides the DNA or RNA, and a body composed of cytoplasm. They function as little chemical factories, producing the chemicals that keep an organism alive.

Chromosomes. Found in pairs in the nucleus of the cell, these structures, composed of proteins and DNA, are the site of genetic activity in higher organisms.

DNA (Deoxyribonucleic acid). The actual material of genes, which control inherited characteristics.

Ecology. The study of the interrelationships between organisms and their environment.

Electron Microscope. Capable of magnifying objects one million times, it uses an electron beam instead of light, and magnetic lenses instead of glass lenses.

Enzymes. A type of protein that aids cellular chemical reactions.

Evolution. A process of chemical and physical changes in organisms that eventually gives rise to new species.

Exobiologist. A scientist who studies the possibility of extraterrestrial life.

Extraterrestrial Life. Any life not native to our earth.

Fossil. Direct evidence of the existence of an organism older than ten thousand years. Such evidence includes petrified bones, preserved footprints, and frozen specimens.

Gene. The element in a cell that controls heredity. Each gene is composed of DNA.

Genetic Code. The system of three-nucleotide sequencing that specifies the amino acid to be added in protein manufacturing.

Genetic Engineering. Manipulation of an organism's DNA to produce a desired result or product.

Genus (plural, genera). A classification grouping, consisting of closely related species.

Greenhouse Effect. The theorized effect in which large amounts of carbon dioxide in the air may trap ground heat and keep it from escaping into space, leading to a rise in the temperature at the earth's surface.

HVEM (High-Voltage Electron Microscope). A microscope that uses a million volts of power to provide large-scale images of chromosomes, reproducing cell nuclei, and three-dimensional views of whole cells.

Insulin. A substance produced by the body that allows it to effectively use glucose. Without it, the sufferer, a diabetic, weakens and dies.

Kingdom. The broadest and most general part of the classification hierarchy. There are five of them: Monera (simple microorganisms such as bacteria), Protista (complex microorganisms such as the amoeba), Plantae (plants), Fungi (mushrooms, molds, and so on) and Animalia (animals).

Mass Extinction. The periodic deaths of large numbers of species, the two greatest having occurred 250 and 65 million years ago.

Messenger RNA. The RNA made by a gene that transfers the genetic information to the ribosomes in protein manufacturing.

Micoorganisms. Living creatures visible only under a microscope.

Mitochondria. Small bodies in a cell that provide, through chemical reactions, energy to the cell and that possess their own DNA.

Mutation. Changes in one or more genes caused by background radiation, mistakes in DNA duplication, and so on.

Natural Selection. The basis for the Darwinian evolutionary theory. Individuals in animal or plant populations who are better adapted to survive a particular environment live longer than those who are not and consequently produce more offspring. After a period of time, these survival traits become part of the entire population.

Nitrogen Bases. Nitrogen-containing compounds attached to either ribose or deoxyribose in DNA and RNA.

Nucleic Acids. The two chemicals—DNA and RNA—responsible for regulating cell activity and reproduction.

Nucleotide. Any of the group of nitrogen compounds linked to a sugar–phosphate backbone, constituting a component of a nucleic acid.

Paleontologist. A scientist who studies fossils.

PKU (Phenylketonuria). A genetic disease whose victims are missing an enzyme needed to break down the chemical phenylalanine. Its toxic effects lead to mental retardation.

Prion. The smallest known organism that may or may not lack any form of nucleic acid and that is responsible for several diseases, among which may be Alzheimer's disease.

Protein. Any of a group of long complex molecules built from amino acids and used as building material within cells.

RNA (Ribonucleic Acid). A molecule that in viruses may be the genetic material, but in most organisms is used in carrying out the directions of DNA in protein manufacturing.

Sociobiology. The study of the relationship between human genes and human culture.

Species. A population of organisms that not only share similar physical and biochemical traits but also can interbreed.

STM (Scanning Tunneling Microscope). A microscope that, instead of lenses, uses a needle-like probe running just above the surface of a specimen to create, through computer-enhancement, a TV image.

Vertebrates. Animals with backbones.

Virus. A very small microorganism whose genetic component is RNA and that uses other cells' genetic material for reproduction.

Z-DNA (Zigzag-DNA). DNA that has nucleotides that stick out, giving the helix a zigzagging appearance. Such a structure may have something to do with determining which genes are activated during protein production.

SELECTED READING

Asimov, Isaac. *A Short History of Biology.* Greenwood, 1980.
Banister, Keith, and Campbell, Andrew, eds. *The Encyclopedia of Aquatic Life.* Facts on File, 1985.
Baskin, Yvonne. *The Gene Doctors: Medical Genetics at the Frontier.* Morrow, 1984.
Bonner, John Tyler. *The Evolution of Culture in Animals.* Princeton University Press, 1983.
Bornstein, Jerry, and Sandy Bornstein. *What Is Genetics?* Messner, 1979.
Breuer, Georg. *Sociobiology and the Human Dimension.* Cambridge University Press, 1983.
Cudmore, L. L. Larison. *The Center of Life: A Natural History of the Cell.* New York Times Books, 1977.
Curtis, Helena. *Biology.* Worth, 1979.
de Duve, Christian. *A Guided Tour of the Living Cell.* Freeman, 1985.
de Rosney, Joel. *Biokit: A Journey to Life.* ADAMA Books, 1984.
Dixon, Bernard. *Magnificent Microbes.* Atheneum, 1976.
Ehrlich, Paul, and Anne Ehrlich. *Extinction: The Causes and Consequences of the Disappearance of Species.* Random House, 1981.
Feinberg, Gerald, and Robert Shapiro. *Life Beyond Earth.* Morrow, 1980.
Freifelder, David. *The DNA Molecule: Structure and Properties.* Freeman, 1978.
Gatston, Arthur W., et al. *The Life of the Green Plant.* Prentice-Hall, 1980.

Gonick, Larry, and Mark Wheelis. *The Cartoon Guide to Genetics.* Harper & Row, 1983.
Gould, Stephen Jay. *The Panda's Thumb.* Morton, 1980.
Hoage, R. J., ed. *Animal Extinctions: What Everyone Should Know.* Smithsonian, 1985.
Hoagland, Mahlon, *Discovery: The Search for DNA's Secrets.* Houghton Mifflin, 1981.
Hoagland, Mahlon, *The Roots of Life.* Avon, 1979.
Lewin, Roger. *Human Evolution: An Illustrated Introduction.* Freeman, 1984.
Life on Earth: A Natural History. Little Brown, 1981.
MacDonald, James Reid. *The Fossil Collector's Handbook: A Paleontological Field Guide.* Prentice-Hall, 1983.
Mackal, Ray P. *Searching for Hidden Animals.* Doubleday, 1980.
McMahon, Thomas A, and John Tyler Bonner. *On Size and Life.* Freeman, 1985.
Margulis, Lynn, and Karlene V. Schwartz. *Five Kingdoms: An Illustrated Guide to the Phyla of Life on Earth.* Freeman, 1981.
Marshall, Kim. *The Story of Life: From the Big Bang to You.* Holt, 1980.
May, John, and Michael Marten. *The Book of Beasts.* Viking, 1983.
Moore, Tui De Roy. *Galapagos: Islands Lost in Time.* Viking, 1980.
Olson, Steve. *Biotechnology: An Industry Comes of Age.* National Academy Press, 1986.
Parker, Sybil P. et al., ed. *Environmental Science.* McGraw-Hill, 1980.
Parker, Sybil P. *McGraw-Hill Dictionary of Biology.* McGraw-Hill, 1985.
Rosenfield, Israel, and Edward Ziff. *DNA for Beginners.* Morton, 1983.
Sattler, Helen Roney. *The Illustrated Dinosaur Dictionary.* Lothrop, 1983.
Scott, Andrew. *Pirates of the Cell: The Story of Viruses from Molecules to Microbe.* Basil Blackwell, 1985.
Shall, N. *Cell Cycle.* Metheum, 1981.

Shapiro, Robert. *Origins: A Skeptic's Guide to the Creation of Life on Earth.* Simon & Schuster, 1986.
Simpson, George Gaylord. *Fossils and the History of Life.* Freeman, 1986.
Stanley, Steven M. *Extinction.* Freeman, 1986.
Stanley, Steven M. *The New Evolutionary Timetable.* Basic Books, 1981.
Stebbins, G. Ledyard. *Darwin to DNA: Molecules to Humanity.* Freeman, 1984.
Steel, Rodney, and Anthony P. Harvey, eds. *The Encyclopedia of Prehistoric Life.* McGraw-Hill, 1977.
Sylvester, Edward J., and Lynn C. Klotz. *The Gene Age: Genetic Engineering and the Next Industrial Revolution.* Scribner's, 1983.
Watson, James D., Tooze, John and Kurtz, David T. *Recombinant DNA: A Short Course.* Scientific American Books, 1983.
Wilford, John Noble. *The Riddle of the Dinosaurs.* Knopf, 1985.
Williams, Roger J., and E. M. Landsford, Jr., ed. *The Encyclopedia of Biochemistry.* Krieger, 1977.

For recent information on biology, consult the following magazines:

Discover
Science News
Scientific American

INDEX

Acid rain, 100–101
Algae, 94–95
Amino acids, 20
    beginning of life and, 70–71
Arctic, species, development of, 65–66
Arizona Barringer Meteorite Crater, 76
Asteroids, mass extinction and, 76–78
Atoms, 14

Biology, 11
    conservation, 106–107
    molecular, 14–16, 17
    population, 16
    sociobiology, 108–115
Biotechnology, 32–33
Burgess Shale fossils, 72

Cancer, 39–40
    interferon, 39
Carbon dioxide, 101
Cells, 11, 17–31
    cytoplasm, 18, 20
    differentiation of, 30–31
    multicelled organisms, 17
    nucleus, 18
    one-celled organisms, 17
    proteins, 20
Chromosomes, 18, 31
Class, 82
Classification system
    (DNA) use in, 86–87
    family, 82
    genus, 82
    kingdoms, 80–81
    order, 82
    phylum, 82
    species, 80
Cold-blooded animals
    characteristics of, 73
    prey to predator ratio, 74
Conservation biology, 106–107
Cooperative behavior, 111–112
Cytoplasm, 18, 20

Diabetes, insulin, 38
Diagnosis, genetic, 40–42
Dinosaurs
    death/disappearance of, 75–78

Dinosaurs *(continued)*
   oldest relic of, 72
   as warm-blooded animals, 73-74
DNA (deoxyribonucleic acid), 20-22, 25, 28-31
   beginning of life and, 70-71
   biological classification and, 86-87
   DNA probe, 41-42
   mitochondrial, 28-30
   mutations, 59-60
   nitrogen bases, 21-22
   nucleotides, 22, 25
   protein manufacturing, 22, 25, 27
   reproduction and, 21-22
   2-DNA, 28

Ecology, 99-107
   conservation biology, 106-107
   pollution, 99
   rainfall/vegetation relationship, 104, 106
   research methods of ecologists, 102-103
   satellite surveys, use of, 103-104
Enzymes, 20, 34
Evolution, 11
   alternate theories, 60, 62
   Darwin's theory, 54, 56, 60
   definition of, 54
   fossil record and, 62-63, 67-68
   harsh environments as spawning grounds, 65-66
   mass extinctions, 67, 79
   molecular level, 58-60
   natural selection, 56-58, 60
   paleontologist's view, 72-73
   theory of evolutionary bursts, 62-64
Extraterrestrial life, 96-98
   exobiologists, 96-97
   planets for exploration, 97-98

Family, 82
Five-Kingdom system, 81
Fossil records
   Burgess Shale fossils, 72
   theory of evolution and, 62-63, 67-68

Genes, 18
   cancer producing, 39-40
   evolutionary change, 58-60
Genetic code, 27
Genetic engineering, 15, 17, 33-44
   dangers from, 36-37
   E. coli bacteria, use of, 33-34, 36
   gene therapy, 44
   genetic diagnosis, 40-42

—125

Genetic engineering *(cont.)*
  genetic disorders, 42–44
  history of, 33
  insulin, 38
  interferon, 39
Genetics, 21
  sociobiology and, 111
Genus, 82
Geothermal heat, lifeforms and, 92–94
Global warming, 101
Greenhouse effect, 101

High-voltage electron microscope (HVEM), 45, 47–48
  3-D images, 49
Human behavior, 110–112
  cooperative behavior, 111–112

Kingdoms, 80–81
  Five-Kingdom system, 81

Life
  beginning of, 69–79
  chemical precursor theory, 70–71
  in tidal pools, 70

MacArthur Portable microscope, 50–51
Mass extinctions, 67
  asteroid hits earth, 76–78
  evolutionary role of, 79
  fossil record data, 75
  volcanic activity and, 78

  weather changes and, 76
Microorganisms, 11
Microscope, 45–51
  compound microscope, 46, 47
  high-voltage electron microscope (HVEM), 45, 46–48
  MacArthur Portable microscope, 50–51
  Scanning Tunneling Microscope (STM), 49–50
  simple, 46
  X-ray viewing, 51–52
Molecular biology, 14–16, 17
Multi-celled organisms, 17
  evolution and, 69
Mutations, 36, 40, 59–60, 87
Myrchison meteorite, 70

Natural selection, 56–58, 60
  criticism of, 60, 62–63
  peppered moth example, 58
  process of, 56, 58
Nitrogen bases, DNA, 21–22
Nucleic acids, 20
Nucleotides, DNA, 22, 25
Nucleus, 18

Ocean, rise of new species, 65
One-called organisms, 17
Order, 82

Paleontologists, 62

—126

Paleontology, advances in, 72
Panda, classification of, 85–86
Phylum, 82
PKU (phenylketonuria), genetic disease, 42–44
Plasmids, 34
Pollution, 99
Ponnamperuma, 70
Population biology, 16
Predators
    evolution and, 72–73
    warm-blooded animals and, 73–74
Primate studies, 108, 112–114
Prions, 95–96
Proteins, 20
    beginning of life and, 70–71
    manufacturing of, 22, 25, 27

Reproduction
    DNA and, 21–22
    prions, 95–96
Reptiles, 79
RNA (ribonucleic acid), 20, 25, 27
    genetic code and, 27
    messenger RNA, 25, 42–43

Sickle-cell anemia, genetic diagnosis, 41
Single-celled organisms, evolution and, 68–69
Sociobiology, 108–115
    basis of, 110
    goal of, 114
    human behavior, 110–112
    primate studies, 108, 112–114
Species, 54
    new, discovery of, 89–98
Sun, life and sunlessness, 90–95

Underwater life
    algae, 94–95
    geothermal heat and life, 90–94

Venus, life forms and, 97
Vertebrates, 56
Viceroy butterfly, evolutionary changes, 63–64
Virus, 40
Volcanoes, mass extinction and, 78

Warm-blooded animals
    characteristics of, 73
    dinosaurs as, 73–74
    prey to predator ratio, 73–74
Weather
    global warming, 101–102
    mass extinction and, 76
    rainfall/vegetation relationship, 104, 106

X-rays, viewing in microscope, 51–52

ABOUT THE AUTHOR

James A. Corrick is editor of *Space Frontier* and *L5 News*, magazines devoted to the future of space travel and colonization. He has written two books, *The Human Brain: Mind and Matter* and *Recent Revolutions in Chemistry*, and published short stories in magazines such as *Chrysalis 6*, *Isaac Asimov's Science Fiction Magazine*, and *Kopernikus 12*. Among his interests are lap swimming and book collecting.